Hope in the Desert

Hope
in the
Desert

CHELSEA BRUNE

Charleston, SC
www.PalmettoPublishing.com

Hope in the Desert
Copyright © 2023 by Chelsea Brune

First Edition

Hardcover ISBN: 979-8-8229-1919-8
Paperback ISBN: 979-8-8229-1920-4
eBook ISBN: 979-8-8229-1921-1

Contents

PART III

Note from the Author

Hey Sweet Sister,

Before you enter into this book, I want you to know that I love you, and so does Jesus. That might sound cheesy, and perhaps even meaningless, but I mean it to the depths of my soul.

I did not want to write this book.

My personal, no-one-asked opinion is that people who write books or put their stuff out there before at least their mid-40s are often prideful, attention-hungry, and unwise. I dislike 95% of things I read by young people. It lacks wisdom, it lacks humility, and it often lacks either biblical Truth or the sweet gift of biblical grace. I certainly didn't (and don't) want to be one of those people. (I promise this book will be nothing if not honest.)

But God has a sense of humor. I wrote this book during years 30 and 31. And most of it was really written (aka lived) in my 20s.

God has been working on my heart for several years convicting me that He's given me experiences that will help other women see that they're not alone – their pain is real, their unseen disappointments hurt, they're not asking questions too big for God, and they aren't forgotten by their Creator. That God is still good amid the mess. That healing can happen.

And I wish someone had been able to tell me all of that in a single book over the last 10 years of my life.

I was lucky – I know women who have walked similar roads, who have been companions in this journey. But sometimes, I needed a safe, quiet, space alone to process some of the real deep pain. And I wanted a voice to speak into that quietness. Quietness that at times felt like a chasm.

I am convinced that these words are not mine. I've seen a glimpse of my Heavenly Father that, for reasons I don't know, He can use. To speak through me, to you. To empower you. To encourage you. To tell you this season isn't hidden from Him. To tell you it's okay to be angry. It's okay to be disappointed. It's okay to be doubled-over in pain. And you are not the only one who has experienced the crap of real life.

He's still for you! And so am I.

I wish I could grab coffee, or a generous glass of my favorite red wine, and talk with you for hours on a comfy couch about this journey. About His faithfulness and love. But also about the deep, deep pain. And the questions I still don't have answers for. And the longings of my heart that are still unfulfilled.

And to tell you as sincerely as I can find words to express, this book isn't about me at all. It's about you. And God's love for you.

It's about Him showing you He sees you. He knows you. He loves you. He hasn't forgotten you. Your questions don't offend Him. Your pain isn't too big for Him.

I'll warn you now – this book doesn't have a finished ending. It's not the story of earthly longings fulfilled. It has unanswered questions. It has messy pieces that are still healing. It has sin that still entangles and ensnares. I'm still praying for a wonderful husband to be by my side.

If you're looking for a book full of happy endings in a clean, neatly assembled package, this book is not for you.

Instead, this book chronicles the honest journey of an imperfect, broken, scared, prideful, messy, beautiful daughter of God. It's the story of a season of the journey that has felt most broken, most unknown, and yet – somehow – has experienced the realness, the goodness, and the heart of God in a way that seasons of calm, and lies of a perfectly packaged life, never produced.

Through the pain, the tears (there have been many), the questions (which have been greater than the tears), the brokenness, and the darkness, God has produced a healing in my heart that I pray continues for the rest of my life.

This is the story of my journey into the heart of God. A heart that is big, is good, and is loving. Not harsh, not legalistic, not cruel. Not cold or distant. A heart that delights in being sought – and seeks out its beloved.

My prayer for you is that this book invites you into the Heavenly Father's heart, whether for the first time or the ten-thousandth. I pray He uses the words on these pages to speak life and truth and love to your heart. He loves you so much! And I pray you feel a touch of that love as we journey together.

In Him – with love and a big hug,

Chelsea Brune

Introduction

This book is broken into three parts.

The first portion covers how we got here. It shares the journey of my initial breaking. A season when I was hit hard by life and overcome with depression, grief and questions that don't have easy answers. It's about a season that changed me forever. It made me less uptight and more compassionate. It showed me darkness doesn't overcome light. It taught me pain won't kill me but needs to be addressed; that wounds often need care.

The second portion encompasses pieces of my journey that I hear echoed in others' journeys. Pieces we haven't heard talked about, or even voiced. Pieces that feel shameful, broken, or just downright confusing. I don't claim to have answers to make them less any less so, but my prayer is that in sharing, you realize you're not alone. That you see that being a Christian doesn't mean having a perfect life and being a God-seeking woman doesn't mean you won't sin or experience disappointment, pain, or evil. Life is messy, and there are not always easy answers to make it better.

The third and final portion of this book is my current. As I type these words, I'm still in the desert of singleness. I haven't seen the biggest earthly desires of my heart come to pass. In fact, life looks nothing like I expected it to at this point. But I have experienced Jesus in this season. And I've learned some lessons in the waiting that are sweet and precious and have grown my hope. I don't have a happy ending yet, but I am walking hand in hand with my Savior and I pray that you see it's possible for you to do so as well, even in the desert seasons.

Part I

MY SLOW UNRAVELING

Chapter 1

Blindsided by an Ending

I was bawling, blinded by tears, and definitely should not have been driving. Minutes earlier my boyfriend of a year and a half had informed me he wasn't sure if he wanted to date me anymore. We were long distance at that point, and he was in town visiting me for our twice a month rotation of weekend visits. We were discussing a plan for our next weekend together, as we hadn't yet booked flights. He was rather quiet, and finally muttered a sentence I wasn't expecting.

"I don't know if we should plan another trip."

He said he wasn't sure he could keep moving forward with me and needed some space to figure things out. And now I was driving him to the airport for his flight back home – in a bewildered state of confusion.

We loved each other. How could he not be sure he wanted to date me anymore? I knew on that drive that we were over, even though we didn't break up that night.

This had come out of left field for me. I thought we were progressing towards marriage. Not a breakup.

I begged him for answers on the drive. "Did I do something wrong?" "Why don't you want to be with me?" "What is wrong with me that makes me so easily discardable?" "Am I unworthy?" "Am I unlovable?"

In time, I'd realize these questions weren't really questions for him. They were questions I had to have answered by one bigger than a human man. They were questions that began a journey of breaking and healing.

I had just turned 28. I had invested a lot of time and energy into this relationship, into this man. And he wasn't sure about me.

This was not my plan.

We had been through a lot in a year and a half, and I thought we'd grown together. He was my best friend, someone I could talk to about anything, someone whose values and beliefs I respected. Someone whose faith I respected. Someone I knew I could weather life's difficulties with because we'd been weathering them throughout our relationship.

On our first date, I found out he had lost his father a few months earlier, and his mother a short two years before that. That news was unexpected. I was keenly aware there was no way in two short months he had properly grieved the loss of his father. But that was not a first date worry.

Sean was very down to earth, intelligent, funny, handsome, and kind. We spent our first date chatting about our views of the world and the church and enjoying a delicious Italian meal. He was an adult, seven years older than me, and I was drawn to his maturity. We enjoyed our first few months of dating, and they felt easy. But that ease was short-lived.

His season was filled with family strife and feelings of unworthiness. There was friction between him and his brothers, which unfortunately boiled to the surface after the loss of both parents. His understanding of his childhood was tainted by this new pain and dysfunction.

A short two months into our relationship, he lost his job unexpectedly. This job loss affected him deeply. He'd had other career disappointments earlier in life, as I'd learn, and was beginning to feel like an eternal screw-up. He then got pulled into an exhausting summer back in his hometown, preparing his childhood home for auction with two brothers who wanted nothing to do with him.

During that season of our relationship, I was navigating a new world of adulthood. I had moved to Omaha for my first job out of law school and loved the adventure but was disappointed by so much relationally. The job wasn't all that it had been sold as, and my boss was inexplicably critical of me. I was away from family and friends and the support system I'd had during seven years in my college town of Bloomington, Indiana, and was navigating making new friends as an adult. Which, it turned out, was much harder than I had expected.

I had been waiting for the day I was out of law school, a contributing member of society, but I was met with a bit of culture-shock realizing that in this new city, a lot of people my age had settled down by their mid-twenties. My entire adult life had been spent in school. I had built-in friend networks because of it. But now, I either had to make friends at work, or I had to find other avenues. The other avenues were confusing and difficult to me. I felt disheartened.

Thankfully, because Sean was older than me, he was kind and honest about the confusion and difficulties that new adulthood brings. I felt comforted and seen in a season of relational discomfort and disappointment.

Sean and I met when we both lived in Nebraska, but my dream after law school was to make it to Colorado. I had taken a job in Omaha with promises that I would be relocated to Denver after a year of training in Omaha. Sean had lived most of his life in Nebraska but had a new opportunity for a great job in Kansas City. So, about 9 months into our relationship, we moved in opposite directions, hundreds of miles apart. And entered new challenges, for each of us individually, and for our relationship.

I relocated to Denver with a new job in what I thought was my dream field. Which quickly proved to be my worst nightmare. My bosses were horrible – something I don't say lightly. I can usually find redeeming qualities in everyone, but years later, I still see none in these two. They were unusually critical, harsh, and downright mean. I was belittled and yelled at. I was constantly questioned as though I was an idiot. And I couldn't get away from it.

I was working 24/7 – literally. I slept with my phone on loud on my pillow. I had not only my cell phone, but my laptop with me at all times. On dates. Going to the grocery store. Going out to dinner with friends. The only boundary I had was to leave the computer in my car during church. But even then, it was only a parking lot away. The joys of high-powered corporate law. I was told I could not take a single vacation day for the first year of the job because we were too busy. But I was burnt out after two weeks.

I was miserable. It was one of the lowest times in my life. I wasn't even two years out of law school and I was wondering if I had made a huge mistake by becoming a lawyer.

This dream I had, this field I had felt called to – it was killing me. I envied baristas and fast-food workers. Anything that wasn't in the field of law. I was ready to quit it forever. Never mind that I had student loans to pay off.

Thankfully, God provided. Through some groundwork I had previously done while searching for this soul-crushing job, I was familiar with a few law firms in Denver that were doing the type of work I had some experience in from my job in Omaha. As it turned out, one of the attorneys I had previously connected with was on the hiring committee of the law firm that happened to have a job opening right as I was desperate to leave this dream-turned-nightmare job.

I got an initial interview, and Sean was my biggest fan. The process was long. Three rounds of in-person interviews over three weeks. From application to job offer took a month. A long month. A grueling month of losing hope. But Sean was confident in God's goodness to me for that season. And after a month of waiting, the job was mine.

I could finally breathe. Two years after graduating law school, I finally felt like a lawyer. And didn't dread it daily.

I thought this was the road back to "normal." I was dating a good man, I finally had a good job, I had made it to my dream city – now for the next steps of marriage and kids.

But God had other plans.

The man left. The city was dark. And my petite frame couldn't hold all of the disappointment, anger, grief, and questions that had been building over the last 28 years.

On that drive, I was completely broken. That drive to Denver Airport was the beginning of my undoing. The second time that the end of Peña Boulevard would lead to the end of a relationship. And the first time I would face the weight of all the disappointment, grief, and unanswered questions the years behind me had brought.

Chapter 2

When Strivings Ceased
... Temporarily

(ALSO KNOWN AS THE FIRST TIME GOD TRIED TO GET ME TO BE OKAY WITH MY BROKENNESS)

My first undoing didn't happen at 28. God had been trying to soften me for years before that drive to the airport where I was doubled over in tears spewing off questions too big for Sean.

I've been ambitious for as long as I can remember. I never needed to be first, or the very best, but always wanted to run with the top of the pack. Coupled with a love of learning and a love of history and government, this ambition led me to law school.

I wanted to go to a top law school. I was aggressive in my applications, knowing for sure I was going to be a "top lawyer" (whatever I thought that meant at 21). My top three law school choices were, in order, the University of Chicago, Georgetown, and the University of Michigan. I was waitlisted at the University of Chicago and Georgetown and flatly rejected by the University of Michigan. I had gone to Indiana University for my undergraduate studies, and applied to its law school, Maurer School of Law, as a "backup." Georgetown interviewed its waitlist candidates and my interviewer happened to be a law professor at Maurer.

So, on a random fall day of my senior year of undergrad, I walked across campus to the law school and met with a Maurer professor. He welcomed me into his office and interviewed me on behalf of his law school alma matter. He gave me a glowing review at the end of our "interview" conversation and said he would relay the same to Georgetown. He then did something unusual, and something that I now attribute to the hand of God in my life.

He took off his "interviewer hat" and wanted to discuss my legal future. He asked where else I was looking. I knew from his resume that he had earned a Ph.D. from the University of Chicago, so we discussed the merits of its law school as well. He asked if I had applied to Maurer. I said I had, but only as a backup. This man I didn't know, who didn't strike me as a salesman, implored me to consider Maurer as more than a backup. He described to me the "temperament" of the law schools I was looking at. The hyper-competition and the stress that would come along with swimming in the most prestigious pools. He was gracious in telling me that if I didn't want to be the absolute best, these schools I had been dreaming of might actually kill me. He recommended I think about what I really wanted long-term and consider if Maurer might have the most benefit for "someone like me." I didn't know then what he meant, but as it turned out, he spoke a heavenly Truth over me that has taken years to accept: I was busy striving – trying to prove myself and carve out a place for myself; meanwhile God was whispering His eternal plans for my abilities, and His place for me.

Law school encompassed some of the best three years of my life. It was the place where, for the first time in my life, not everything came easy. I actually had to study. A lot. I had to do more than read a chapter once. And as I was reading cases which I wouldn't be tested on until the semester's end, I had no barometer to know whether I was actually learning anything or not.

I loved the challenge! After my first semester of my first year of law school I felt like I had finally found my place. I felt challenged and I was surrounded by high achievers. As it turns out, most people who go to law school are pretty smart, and usually **very** ambitious. Instead of feeling like the "smart" one, I was now one of many.

Actually, I looked relatively average – and felt as much for the first time in my life. Which I found refreshing. I loved my peers. Some are still the people I consider my "law school fam" – people who have seen my best and worst and have loved me in spite of myself.

I had always been pretty healthy and had a "good head on my shoulders" growing up. I was usually considered the "stable" one of my friend groups. I was never prone to major shifts in temperament. I remember crying in the theater during P.S. I Love You when I was in high school. I was with my best friends who'd known me my whole life and they all looked horrified – they'd never seen me shed a tear and were anxious to make sure I was okay. I didn't cry often back then. I prided myself on being "controlled" and "collected." I liked that part of me. It felt safe. And stable.

But God didn't think that part of me was as necessary or noble as I did.

During fall break of my first semester of law school, I had a massive panic attack on I-69 on my drive home from Bloomington, which left me shaking and seizing on the floor of a rest stop in the middle of Indiana. That night, my angels were a group of long-haul truckers who took turns talking to me, making sure I was still conscious, and getting me liquids, while I waited for my parents to make the hour and a half drive from my home to the rest-stop where I had pulled over as the seizures got really bad.

It was the most out of control I had ever felt in my life. I watched my legs and arms literally shake uncontrollably as my heart felt like it was beating outside of my chest. I had no idea what was wrong with me. And no idea how to calm my body down. I had never had seizures before.

It was a completely unsettling event for a control freak like me. Even worse for one who liked being "put together." Here I was, writhing on the floor in front of complete strangers – how embarrassing! My parents got there and took me home but the convulsions didn't stop, except in bits and spurts as I slept.

I spent the next week of fall break going to the doctor to figure out what was wrong with me. I was prepared for a diagnosis of disease, but not the one I got. "Anxiety," said the physician assistant. "Your blood work all came back normal, and the only remaining explanation is that you have generalized anxiety."

'What? No, excuse me, there must be a mistake. I don't have anxiety. I'm not nervous about things. I'm stable,' I thought. 'How could I have anxiety?'

The physician assistant recommended an anti-depressant to help even out my brain chemicals. Since I have a history of mental illness in my family, my mom was able to suggest which medicine we try as much of my family had benefitted from it already.

I now see how much of a weird blessing this was. Anti-depressants can be a godsend, but there's still a lot about the science of our brains that doctors don't know. Because of this, sometimes, which medicine to prescribe for anxiety and depression is truly a guessing game. I have friends who have suffered the ills of medicines that don't work well, and even make the problem worse. I was lucky. Once we got the dosing right, this medicine seemed to stop the constant flood of feeling like I was on hyper-alert and might any minute break into shaking.

But, as my doctor kindly explained, "this medicine will not take away your anxiety, but it will give you the ability to fight it from a 'normal' place, instead of getting sucked into the panic attacks. It will take work to learn healthier patterns of thinking and know how to talk yourself down." Great, I thought. So there's something wrong with my brain, and I'm not in control, but I also have to keep working to make it better? Lovely.

The next few months were extremely uncomfortable. I wanted to go back to "normal." I wanted the medicine to just let me return to how I had always functioned. I felt like my brain had betrayed me. No matter how "in control" I had tried so hard to be, my brain chemicals didn't care.

Honestly, I felt like God betrayed me, too. How was I going to be a lawyer if I couldn't make it through law school? How was I going to make it through law school if I couldn't think straight?

I knew it wasn't law school that had triggered this completely. There were unresolved hurts of the past seasons of life that came barreling down all at once during this new season of change. It had been too much for my subconscious mind to handle on top of the mental rigors of law school, and my body reacted. (I'd later learn that our minds can only hold so much until unresolved emotions evidence themselves in our physical bodies.)

My idea of "normal" and "control" had gone out the window. I was not as "stable" as I had always prided myself on being. I realized I did not have complete "control" over my brain or my thoughts. I now had an impediment to my "stability" called anxiety.

And yet, even in that season, anxiety became a blessing. One of many times in my life that God allowed what I did not want to save me from a path I thought I did.

I wanted to be a "top lawyer" and achieve greatness in the eyes of my profession. I'll admit here that I actually wanted to be a Supreme Court Justice when I first entered law school. To do so, you must be a standout – from law school throughout your career. And in part thanks to my unexpected anxiety starting my first semester of law school, I wasn't a standout.

I was not at the top of the class. In fact, I was nowhere close. When I went to law school, only Ivy League educated lawyers had ever sat on the modern Supreme Court bench, and I wanted to do everything in my power to set myself up to be one of them. I had already wrestled with God over going to Maurer – finally relenting to the fact that if He wanted me to sit on the Supreme Court, He could place me there no matter where I went to law school. (I'm super nerdy but super serious – this was my real dream back then.)

At the time, I honestly thought this was all the surrender I would need to muster for my vision of my future. Naïve, I know. But as I rounded out my first semester of law school, I was starting to realize my vision of my future might need to be re-adjusted.

I was extremely blessed to be at Maurer for this season. In case you are unfamiliar with law school, it's competitive. Really competitive. And in many cases, cut-throat. Because all grading is on a curve, your classmates doing worse means you do better. There's not an "objective" A. There is you compared to everyone else. (So much for not comparing yourself to others.) Because of this grading mechanism, there's an incentive to hoard your resources.

Your primary learning tool in law school is the notes you take in class. At most law schools, missing a class means missing out. This is a competition after all. If you didn't take notes or show up, everyone else gets a leg up on the curve.

Maurer was different. As may be obvious from the above, you are not supposed to miss class. Especially in your 1L year. But I remember one random day, my anxiety was overwhelming, and I emailed my professor letting him know I wouldn't make it to class. He was kind and asked me if I wanted to meet with him separately to go over the materials. That doesn't happen in law school! If that wasn't enough, multiple classmates emailed and txt me to share their notes. I cannot emphasize enough; this is not typical. Or at least wasn't in the days I went to law school. But God was providing. Even with my anxiety.

My plans for my future started to relax. With a **heavy** emphasis on "started to." I would like to say that my introduction to anxiety led to tremendous healing. But if I'm honest, it merely opened the window to begin allowing it. I still wanted "stable." I still wanted "normal." I still wanted the life I had planned. I did not want messy. I did not want broken. I did not want unknowns. I spent the next three years of law school in a wrestling match with God over how much brokenness and mess were supposed to be allowed a place in my life.

Perhaps it's a testament to how stubborn I am that seizures on the side of the road, anxiety, and seeing God's hand of provision weren't enough to get my focus off the picture of life I had in my head, but I doubt I'm alone. We think of the pieces of our lives that are "off-track" as detours from the straight-line destination we have in our heads. But God sees them as part of the journey. As it turns out, the journey He is ultimately concerned with isn't what law school I graduated from or what my career looked like. While He does care about those things, they aren't the ultimate things I often make them. He is primarily focused on my journey into His heart. And that journey was just beginning.

Chapter 3

Initial Heartbreak

I met Daniel a few weeks after my initial bouts with anxiety. He went to law school with me and had the guts to ask me out. The first guy to truly do so in my first 23 years of life.

My parents wisely did not let my sister or me "date" until we were 16. By 16, I realized I did not want to date anyone I was in school with. Not because of them – I grew up with a lot of really good Christian guys – but because I had much bigger plans than most of my peers. (Recall, I sincerely wanted to be a Supreme Court Justice.)

I was from a tight-knit community in Indiana where I went to high school with the same kids I had known in pre-school. And lots of people stayed there. Went to one of the local colleges and then got jobs in that community. I didn't understand that then. I was dying to get out and see the world. And I did not want to be with someone who didn't share my desire for adventure. Besides, I had a vision – I was going to law school

– and nothing and no one was going to stand in my way of that.

My first four years of college entailed more singleness. There were a few serious crushes here and there, but nothing that materialized into anything more. I was at a state school, so fellow Christians were far less numerous than they had been where I grew up. I also found that many of the Christians I met during undergrad were newer believers who were a little too green and a lot too pushy about their faith.

I wanted to be a witness for God in a professional setting. Having been blessed to grow up in a Christian home where we were strongly encouraged to find our own faith footings, I had a heart for people "like me." The smart, logical, driven types. I knew that if I hadn't been exposed to Christianity early in life, I would have a lot of questions. (Heck, I did and still do, despite being exposed early.) I also knew that I wouldn't want people telling me what I needed. I would have been attracted to Christianity by people. People who did life with me. Who did life differently, better. People who cared about others more than they focused on themselves. That was the call on my heart for ministry in my 20s.

So, unsurprisingly, I was single as I entered law school. While I was admiring which classmates were cute, I was not actually thinking about dating. I had to focus. Besides, with anxiety as a new companion, I had more than enough to handle.

At this point in my life, I had also begun to wear a label – I was "a lot." No, no, not in a bad way, I was always assured. But I had "a lot" going for me. I was a Christian, committed to living for Christ. I was a smart, ambitious female who was going to law school. I was extroverted and social. And I was not completely ugly. Apparently, those things together make a woman "a lot."

So, I had begun to accept that it would take a "special" man to partner with me. In my early 20s, this still felt like more of an invitation to greatness. Good things come to those who wait, right?

Along came Daniel.

Daniel didn't care that I was a lot when he asked me out. Actually, he tricked me into a date.

He had lost a bet (one which he instigated) during a weekly law school happy hour. Loser had to buy the next round. This is typical law school camaraderie, and I thought nothing of it until he told me he was not paying up there, in the college bar where drinks were $2. He proposed to pay up that Saturday, at a much nicer place. So, we had our first date that weekend, with fancy cocktails instead of $3 long islands.

He talked. A LOT. I'm not the type of girl to sit quietly and listen to someone blabber on out of politeness. (I'm sure my mother is rolling her eyes reading this and wishing sometimes I would hush a bit more.) But Daniel mesmerized me.

Daniel was equal parts confident (bordering on cocky), smart, adventurous, and ambitious. He was a fellow Hoosier but had already left the state, returning for law school after going to college on the East Coast, traveling the world, and more. He was a Christian – and seemed normal. (Which should be far more prevalent than it is, but let's be honest, sometimes Christians are weirdos.) Daniel came from a big family and his parents were still together. He shared my views on a lot of things, and so I sat listening to this man for hours.

After I got home from our date, Daniel txt me to apologize. He noticed that he had talked my ear off and was sorry he hadn't taken time to get to know me better. He asked if I would meet him for breakfast the next morning before church. I was surprised by his self-awareness, and flattered by his eagerness, so I said yes.

I don't remember exactly when we were "officially dating" but we quickly settled into a relationship. I thought he was everything I had dreamed of and waited for – Christian, smart, ambitious, handsome, athletic, funny (with an infectious laugh). Though he had a healthy ego to the outside world, he was sweet and kind to me. And was head-over-heels for me.

He didn't think I was "a lot" – he thought I was wonderful. He didn't care that I had anxiety and was super patient with me as I navigated life with this new disease. Anxiety got me to slow down enough to notice this guy, and I found someone who would be a great partner – a shared faith, an understanding of my ambition, and an intellectual equal. Perhaps God had allowed my anxiety *for* this reason – to get my focus off of my goals long enough to find my future husband.

I thought I had it all figured out. God allowed brokenness because I was stubborn and driven and He needed to unblind me at just the right time. Good job God!

Because I hadn't dated until Daniel, I also hadn't experienced the thrills of a first kiss. I never actually admitted that to Daniel, but he knew, and didn't push me until I was ready. Which was two months into dating (poor guy). But one night I was ready, and I finally found out what the fuss was about and was a big fan.

We set physical boundaries early, as I was adamant about saving sex for marriage. But kissing and cuddling were still on the table.

I was new to physical intimacy of any kind and found new aspects of my femininity being unearthed by Daniel's affection. I knew I was decent looking, but I had never known the affection and delight of a man in a relationship. I began to discover how it made my soul sing. I saw how being delighted in gave me a sense of security and made me feel like I was walking on air.

But I also became aware of the exposure that physical intimacy outside of marriage can bring. It awakened new desires and flirted with satisfying others. It left me thrilled. But it also left me raw. A more intimate kind of raw than I had previously known. I was more vulnerable than ever. I had given Daniel something I had never given anyone else, something I never could – my firsts. I realized in giving him parts of my sexuality, I was forced to trust him, not only with my body but also with my heart and soul. And that left me exposed.

As I was discovering the realities of the connection between my sexuality and my soul, Daniel and I were also negotiating our vision for our future. I say negotiating because we were both in law school, so rigorous debate was part of our relationship. We both had ideas on what life afterward should look like. But his were a little more set than mine (which is saying something because I'm nothing if not strong-willed).

I didn't know when we started dating that Daniel came from money. Lots of money. The kind of money where his dad had owned a private jet when Daniel was a kid, because how else would he have been able to attend all his work meetings and still have made it home in time for baseball practice? That kind of money.

I was uncomfortable with this level of wealth. I had not grown up poor, nor did I think I ever really would be (I was going to law school after all), but I had never aspired to that level of wealth. Quite frankly, it felt like too much. Like surely if you love Jesus, you give most of your money away if you're that rich? (A notion I don't subscribe to in the same way years later but still firmly believe the love of money is the root of all sorts of evil.)

Daniel was the first son, the heir apparent to his father and grandfather's business legacies. He didn't have to apply for a job after law school. He had one. Some trust fund kids (as they're kindly referred to) are lazy, mooching off money they've never worked for. That was not Daniel.

Daniel was relentlessly ambitious. Which I found incredibly attractive. But which I also started to see, would forever impact my life. His dad owned a private jet because he was gone 3-4 days a week for most of Daniel's childhood. Daniel's mom had graciously and lovingly held down the fort with 6 kiddos. And a nanny. And Daniel's expectation was to follow in his father's footsteps.

I remember when he first shared this expectation with me at dinner one night. I had never met someone with such a narrow vision of their future. I mean, don't get me wrong, it was a big plan, which was seemingly admirable. But it didn't leave a lot of room for "us" to grow and discover a life together. It placed me into a role, a path, and a life, that I wasn't sure I wanted. I had grown up with a stay-at-home mother, and I am deeply thankful for that gift. It's one that I hope to give my children in some form. But I also wanted a career.

I wanted Daniel. But did I want the life he had planned?

It was a question I struggled with. Moreso because Daniel entered the family business while we were in law school. He started living the life his father had modeled before him. He traveled almost weekly and was only in law school to pick up a degree. So I was left to figure it out.

"I don't know how to do this. I don't know how to not feel neglected when Daniel leaves. I don't know how to not feel like I'm just a convenient piece of arm candy to him. I don't know how to not feel uncared for. Daniel is pretty dang sure this is his life, and so the burden is on me to get good at it. But this feels so unfair. It seems unloving that he could say our relationship comes down to our ability to make his job fit our lives. My ability to get comfortable with it. I know I'm called to support and love a husband but that's hard to do when I feel him not pursuing me as he once did but pursuing his business oh so well."

While Daniel had pursued me well during the first few months of our relationship, I had caught him in a brief lull – in between carefree student and serious business guy. Once the business hat went on, things changed. At the same time, I loved him. And he loved me. So, while I was still pursuing my own degree and my own career, law school became a secondary focus. I was focused on trying to figure out if I could become the supportive wife, and woman, that Daniel wanted.

In asking myself if I could be that woman, I also started to ask if this was the kind of marriage or "love" I wanted – one where I did the work to fit into someone else's life.

As I asked myself numerous questions, I also started to turn the questions back on him. If he loved me, couldn't we start a new plan, or at least do life differently than his parents had, since we, not them, were going to live our lives? We argued about his work and his goals a lot. The same ambitious nature that had drawn me to him initially became a flash-point of our fights. Because I knew his exact goals, from the number of businesses he wanted to own to the amount of money he wanted to make, it was easy to see how much work it would take to get there. And how much sacrifice it would be for his wife.

We also fought about the fact he was going into a family business. I wasn't the biggest fan of his dad. I didn't have words for it then, just an intuition that while I loved Daniel, I could not marry his father. Which presented a problem.

Daniel's role model in life and business was his father. And it was his father's money that funded the family business. Thus, it would be his father who forever made decisions about Daniel's work, and therefore, our life.

Let me sidebar here: I am not against money. Even lots of money. I have a career as a lawyer and make, what I consider to be, a lot of money. Money is not the problem. A love of money is. And it was a love of money that I saw in Daniel, and in his father, early on. A discernment that was too big for my little frame. A knowledge too wise for my young years. It was the Spirit of God whispering Truth to me.

Truth that came to a head in the beautiful mountains of Colorado one Fourth of July. Daniel's family had a second home outside of Vail. It was as large and immaculate as you might expect. The first time I went, my jaw hit the floor when we pulled in. It was extravagant. And I could not believe people lived like this in real life.

Daniel and I were in the middle of our second summer of distance, the summer after my second year of law school. I was at a summer internship, and he was running a business multiple states away. While there was underlying discord about how to create a life together given the tight parameters his vision (and his family) allowed, we loved each other and were pretty certain we would get married. So even with distance, we spent as many weekends together as we could (which is easier to do with a lot of money).

Just a week before, we had flown to New York City to go to his friend's engagement party. Beforehand, he took me to the fanciest steak dinner I'd ever had, and I got to wear the prettiest party dress I think I ever will. The morning after, he announced that we were going ring shopping. At Tiffany's.

While this should have been a fairytale moment, it wasn't.

Rings had become another sore spot for us. He came from money – and his mother, aunt, and all the married women in his circle had rings that evidenced the same. Please understand, no one has ever accused me of being modest. In fact, my jewelry choices can often be described as gaudy.

But Daniel's desire to show off his money with my engagement ring felt wrong. It seemed he was not trying to give me the world, but was trying to show the world that he could buy anything. Hence, Tiffany's.

We had already talked about rings, and I had an idea of what I wanted. A unique style that Tiffany's did not offer. But after brunch, Tiffany's is where we went.

It was one of the most out-of-place, unfun experiences I've ever had. (Not a good sign for engagement ring shopping with the love of your life.) Daniel kept insisting I try on rings that were huge and expensive, and made both the salespeople and I raise our eyebrows. I tried to oblige him, but eventually got him to take the hint that my engagement ring wasn't at Tiffany's. He finally agreed we could leave, but before we did, he wanted to look at the floor where they sold expensive watches – one like his dad had. We spent more time at the watch counter than we did with the diamonds. By about three-fold. To say I was miffed is an understatement.

I was beginning to feel like status, money, and being better than his dad mattered more to Daniel than I did.

But I stuffed that feeling away. Along with all of my other doubts and fears about our relationship, his ambition, and his family dynamics. Until one evening the reality of my fears came crashing down.

Half the family had made it to Colorado for the Fourth of July, including Daniel and myself. We hiked, swam, played yard games, and were having a great time, until the second evening at dinner.

Daniel had mentioned early on in our relationship that his dad's lawyers were advising him that the kids should all sign pre-nups when they got married. I was in law school at the time, so I understood the legal benefits of a pre-nup. A lawyer's job is to protect you from risk. Because so many marriages end in divorce, marriage is a risk to your assets from a purely legal standpoint.

But I want God-honoring, covenant commitment, not a contractual marriage. Did then, still do. I told Daniel early on that I would not sign anything except a marriage certificate to marry him. He said that was fine, and I thought that was the end of it.

I was sorely mistaken.

That night at dinner, the conversation somehow turned to pre-nups. I thought Daniel had talked to his dad about the same since we were talking about engagement. How wrong I was.

Daniel's father told me in no uncertain terms that I was naïve to be in law school and not understand the need for a pre-nup. He became so angry he left dinner early, something I had never seen him do. Daniel sat silent as others at the table tried to explain his father's anger and assuage the situation. At some point, I excused myself from dinner and went back to my room.

I was seeing red. I had never been as angry as I was in that moment. Because at that dinner I realized two equally horrifying things. Money, not Jesus, was king in this family and Daniel was never going to stand up to his father. The weight of the two realities colliding in my mind, and that present moment, were too much.

When Daniel walked into my room I was bawling. And once I saw him, I was yelling. I couldn't believe he had sat silent. I couldn't believe he didn't defend me to his father. I couldn't believe he had never mentioned our decision on pre-nups to his father while we were talking about marriage and actively ring-shopping.

In that room, I realized I was alone. In this house and in this relationship. The man I thought I could trust didn't stand up for me when I needed him to, didn't fight for me, didn't defend me.

I insisted Daniel take me to a hotel. He told me that was awkward and would make the situation worse. I did not budge. I would walk there if I needed to. He relented and went to a hotel with me.

We argued most of the night but by morning he had somehow convinced me that his parents would come around, and while yes, they were in the wrong, if we wanted to build a life together, we had to be the bigger people and try to bridge the gap and go back for the rest of the weekend.

This time I relented. After all, I loved this man and while I had just been betrayed by his silence and seen his father's true colors to be exactly what I feared, sleep deprivation and stress aren't known as a winning combination for great decisions. So we went back for the next two days of the long weekend. And danced around the issue mostly.

On Sunday afternoon, Daniel and I finally had time alone while he drove me to the airport. We argued the whole drive from Vail to the airport in Denver (with traffic, it was a fun 3 hours). I was pretty sure we were breaking up, but he begged me not to. He loved me and wanted to build a life with me and swore we'd figure this out.

The next day I was back in Indiana and he was off to meetings with his dad. When he called, he had only 15 minutes because he had to go back to work. That was the kiss of death.

He wasn't going to address my concerns, let alone my needs, because he was too busy working. In that moment I saw his priorities were money and success, and those two would always come before me. I broke up with him on the phone. He swore he'd fight to be the man I could marry and would win me back. I wanted to believe him, but something in me knew it was over.

Chapter 4

Letting Go ... When Forced

*D*aniel and I broke up in between our second and final year of law school. Which meant two equally horrifying things: 1) I had to go back to school with him for a year; and 2) all of my friends and classmates (and sadly, even professors) got to watch me in the aftermath of my first real breakup.

I was not emotionally prepared for either of those things. Nor was I prepared for the wrestle with God that this breakup had invited.

If it's not clear by now, I wanted my life to be neat and tidy. I had grown up seeing plenty of hardship and trauma within my own extended family and in the lives of people around me, so I didn't think life would be perfect. But I had only considered the "worst-case" tragedies – death, disease, and disability. I had no idea how deeply relational trauma could affect a person. Sure, I'd had friends come and go over the years, but it wasn't that big of a deal. (Actually, I'd later find out it was a big deal, one I had been too busy to realize.)

But this loss of relationship, my breakup with Daniel, it paralyzed me. It took both the person I loved the most, and all expectations I had for my future away – all in an instant. It was crushing.

For as much as Daniel and I had never fully settled on how our lives would look after law school, my view of my future was certain on two things: 1) Daniel would be my husband, and 2) we would live in Colorado. Post breakup, I had no direction, and no companion. I also had less than a year to figure out a new plan with law school coming to an end. While figuring out a plan for post-graduation was heavy on my mind, I came to see it was the least of my real problems.

For as much of a planner as I was, I didn't anticipate that a breakup could cause me so much pain.

But there was a lot of pain packed into this one. First, it was my first real relationship – and had lasted a year and a half – through the toughest season I had faced up to that point. Second, it had been serious, and was headed towards marriage. Those kinds of breakups hurt deeply. When you've done the work to start considering and planning for a life together and together ends before it begins, it's traumatic. Third, it had disrupted my plan. While I think I'm fairly flexible in most things, I used to be pretty fixed on long-term plans. And didn't take kindly to disruptions. Finally, Daniel really had checked all the boxes of what I thought I wanted and needed in a spouse at the time. And I had waited so long (or what I thought was so long back then) for that kind of man. And he actually loved me. And had sought me out.

Why would God let that fail? Why hadn't God just changed Daniel's heart to want God, me, and then a career – in that order?

I hadn't had to ask questions of God on such a personal nature before. Yes, I'd seen tough things in my extended family and in my friends' lives, but my concept of God hadn't yet been totally unsettled. While I knew God wasn't one of equations, I really believed that if I picked a man who met my criteria – loved Jesus, had a shared worldview, loved me, and had ambition, the rest would automatically fall into place.

How wrong I was.

My final year of law school is honestly a bit of a blur. In part because of how blurred my vision was through all the tears. In part because I walked around in a fog as my thoughts and emotions swirled. And in part because of how much alcohol I consumed. I'm not proud of the plentiful alcohol consumption. But I was hurting. And I wanted to numb the pain. And stop feeling so sad. I had never cried so much in my life. It's like the tears just wouldn't stop. I couldn't find the "off" switch.

I just couldn't make sense of it. I didn't understand how someone could carry the name of Jesus and profess His kind of love … and leave. Or just give up, really. That part honestly probably made me spiral more than the sadness of that breakup.

I'm loyal to a fault. So someone giving up just did not compute in my brain. I couldn't make sense of the hypocrisy and selfishness that was the reality of Daniel's heart. I'm no saint (see above), but I also hate inconsistency in people. And in myself. And had a lot less grace for both back then.

While I was facing the reality of who Daniel was, I was still begging God to change his heart. In part because I still loved him.

But I can see now, mostly because my view of God's abilities were quite small. (They still are, but I'd like to think they're gradually increasing.) I thought I had met the man of my dreams. Since I couldn't change Daniel (which took me all too long to realize), I decided the only other option was that maybe I needed to step back and let God change him.

Yes, surely this was the plan now! God would allow some breaking (because all good stories have struggles), and then we'd be reunited and life would go swimmingly. I'm embarrassed to admit, I spent up through my law school graduation honestly hoping for this. My friends thought I was nuts. (Because I was.) But mercifully loved me anyway.

The worst part of my grand delusion of a miraculous reconciliation is that Daniel in many ways played along with it. The first time I saw him post-breakup was once we were both back in Bloomington before school started. We did a typical post-breakup "return of things." I went to his apartment and saw the saddest version of him I'd ever witnessed. He immediately hugged me with tears in his eyes, and I had to back up and say "no – you don't get to do that anymore."

I was not prepared for that. He had barely spoken to me the rest of the summer after the 'fireworks' of the Fourth of July. I was convinced (and terrified) that he'd already moved on. To see him so broken, clearly still missing me, too – it sparked hope. It's honestly probably where the grand delusion of reconciliation really took hold.

For the next year, we still had classes together, still had mutual friends, and still chatted semi-regularly. I'll admit, I was the one pushing to chat. I wanted to see him. I wanted things to go back to normal. We even had "dates." While I wouldn't go out in public with him (because it was a small college town and I didn't want people to see us together if we weren't actually … yet), he had me over and made me dinner multiple times. I recall one evening of such a dinner that fall. Out of nowhere, Daniel blurted out "this was supposed to be the happiest season of our lives – we were supposed to be engaged and excited about the future."

Not fair! My soft, hopeful, female heart couldn't process those words without believing it meant there was still hope. And I white-knuckled the rest of the school year wanting to believe God would reunite us.

But that wasn't God's plan. It was Chelsea's. While it was partly my plan because I still loved Daniel, it was partly my plan because I wanted to avoid more pain. More singleness seemed to suggest more pain. Trying to find another man seemed to suggest more struggle. This was the neatest, tidiest solution my brain could come up with – it was reconciliation with Daniel or bust.

But in His infinite wisdom, God didn't get on board with Chelsea's plan. Because He has a better plan. Daniel and I never got back together. God actually had to jolt me into that reality by letting me accidentally run into Daniel on a date the evening of graduation. (I'm telling you, I held on hard.) Until that moment, I still really thought God would bring us back together (and thought Daniel's lack of moving on all year had meant the same). As it turns out, he'd probably moved on long before this date, but had kept me from that knowledge.

I was shattered all over again. But looking back, I'm thankful God pried this out of my hands.

I hate to admit this, but I think sometimes letting us get shattered is the kindest thing God can do. Knowing what I know now, I would rather still be single than have been married to Daniel and white-knuckled marriage to a man whose convictions did not align with mine. I'm thankful that as my ambitions, heart, and even pace have changed over the years after law school, I didn't have to bristle against a husband (and extended family) who had a very set view of who I was supposed to be and how I was supposed to act. I'm thankful God gave me space to grow into myself apart from any man, but especially thankful that I wasn't hitched to Daniel during this past season of growth.

Because my views have changed. Ambition in a man is still somewhere on my list, but its definition changed. Though I'm still a lawyer in a corporate setting, I couldn't care less if my future husband runs in the same circles. To be honest, I barely fit in those circles anymore – or perhaps never really did. I don't want a man who is chasing things of this world. I want a man who is chasing Kingdom things.

So God had to force me to let go. He had to pry my hands open. To get me to let go of what I thought I wanted. To invite me into more than I dreamed of. To invite me on a grand adventure with Him.

Chapter 5

Learning to Be Broken

I considered myself pretty put together when I was young. I counted it a virtue. I actually have a vivid memory of being in the church basement where our youth group met, and thinking during a worship song, "where are suitable role models?" "None of these people are living up to what they say their faith means to them, and none of them are heading in a similar direction in life as I am." First of all, holy pride! I know. But sadly, I have realized that in that moment, I subconsciously decided it was my job to be a role model. A role model to whom, I'm not exactly sure. But I so valued this "put-together" virtuous person that seemed to be lacking in my life that somewhere in my teenage brain, I promised myself to be that for someone else.

Having role models, and even being a role model is a wonderful thing. But I made it ugly. In my mind it was supposed to be someone who lived up to their calling, someone who never disappointed, and someone whose life was not a mess. I would not say I was a perfectionist, but I had very high standards, mostly for myself.

I was a church kid, so I knew sin had ruined Eden. I knew that life on earth would have trouble. I had seen bad things happen to good people plenty. I had seen tragedy strike indiscriminately in the lives of people who were faithful followers of God and those who were not. I knew that could happen. And perhaps because of that awareness, even at a young age, I wanted to control something. I wanted to have some say in how much tragedy and strife was allowed to enter my life.

Somewhere along the line, I saw that while I could not control external circumstances, I could control myself. I could "avoid" the "extra consequences" of sin through good behavior. I seriously thought that if I did the right things, I could control how much brokenness would happen in my heart, and my life. Underneath that belief was deep fear – fear that brokenness would separate me from everyone, including God – fear that I was not strong enough to bear the weight of brokenness. And by my mid-20s, those fears were uncovered for what they were: pride and a deep distrust of God's goodness and mercy.

I had subconsciously come to believe that I needed to earn God's love. That sounds crazy for a girl who grew up in the evangelical church – I knew that I was saved by grace alone. But can I be honest? I didn't think I needed that much grace. I thought I was pretty okay and just needed that extra boost of Jesus' blood to get into heaven. I had self-control and discipline and had a good handle on life. While I did not consciously structure my life around this belief, it was there, underneath the surface, and as it turns out, it guided a lot of what I did.

That is part of why my anxiety in law school came as such a shock – it shook my identity. As it turns out, a large part of my identity was in being "put together." It was much harder to be "put together" when my brain was falling apart.

Another major piece of my identity had become rooted in my strivings to be excellent. Excellent at school, and later, at work. An excellent friend. An excellent girlfriend. An excellent leader. An excellent mentor. An excellent woman – pretty enough without trying too hard, a gracious host, an excellent cook. I wanted to be all things to all people. I knew I could not be great at everything (I am never going to be an Olympic athlete), but I wanted to be great at the things I was engaged in.

I was striving.

"STRIVING … that's what has recently defined many of my relationships – with You, with friends, with family. When I lack, I believe that lacking is a reflection on me."

I remember those words hitting me like a ton of bricks as I penned them after a counseling session with a woman who was the epitome of cold who had come recommended by my church at the time. I didn't continue seeing her (yes, it's okay/normal to try out a few counselors before you find the right fit). But I am forever thankful for the wheels she set in motion in August of 2018. Because she was right. I was killing myself striving to "earn" love.

I did not know then that two months later Sean and I would break up. Nor that it was the beginning of a journey into my own brokenness. It wasn't just on that drive to the airport that I cried.

It was every day. For months. But the tears were grieving more than just the end of that relationship.

God decided this was the time to open the floodgates of my heart – to expose years of junk that had built up within its walls. Disappointment, misplaced hopes, lies I believed about myself and Him, family wounds, shattered expectations, dashed dreams – they all came flooding in through the opening of this breakup. And came rushing down my face in tears that were too heavy for me.

I found I no longer had the strength to be ashamed of this mess. I had no energy to put on a good face. By the grace of God, after that cold counselor, I found an amazing counselor named Christine a few weeks before Sean and I broke up and this dam of emotion broke. I frequently sat in Christine's office struggling to put words together with a face covered in tears and a heart that felt like it fell out of my chest.

I wanted it to end. I wanted a fix for this pain. I wanted to get out of it, around it, through it – to put it behind me quickly. And I remember Christine kindly telling me that a quick fix was not likely. (Why was I paying her again?)

God was whispering Truth to my heart about the purpose for this season as well.

"Chelsea, what if this isn't about testing or pain? What if this is really extravagantly about healing? What if I've allowed this space to weed out the toxic lies you believe, to heal the scars you've lived with and gotten used to? What if this isn't cruel, what if it's kind?"

Years later, I can say that God unraveling me into a vulnerable woman who isn't (completely) afraid of her own weakness was a gift. A gift I'm still unwrapping – still learning how to use. Because brokenness is not a one-time thing. The thing that feels the most broken this year may be healed next year. And in ten years, a broken thing that you never imagined might emerge. Following God is not a guarantee that pain can be avoided. In fact, I think the Biblical record and my own life experiences thus far would suggest that following God is an invitation to pain. Not because God is cruel. But because Satan is real. The good news of the Gospel is the pain will end. Satan has already been defeated. Heaven promises us no more tears.

But while we're still in these flesh-suits, I think God often gives us time to be "in" the broken to discover His love there. In the brokenness. I wrote these words in my season of unraveling.

"I still need time to heal, but perhaps moreso, time to discover who You really are when I'm not striving. When I feel unseen, unimportant. Are You good to me here? Not good once it ends – once I'm in a relationship, not once I'm healed – are You good here, in the brokenness, in the sadness, in the pain, in the unknown? I know in my head the answer is "yes". Speak that to my soul. Gently show me Your love here – in this hidden season. I have no large work accomplishments. I have no relationship to tout. I don't have a next adventure to show off. I have You. And I know You're hiding me in that – but that sometimes feels like a curse, not a blessing. Give me Your generous, unearned, extravagant love. Meet me here. Before the "next" thing."

I was striving to "earn" love and acceptance, so in His mercy, one of the most gracious things God could do was let me sit in the brokenness and experience His acceptance in its midst. I needed to unlearn my association with "deserving" love and "receiving" it. I needed to see God loved me just as much when I was a mess as He did when I was crushing it.

As a life-long Christian, and one who didn't step far out of line growing up, I honestly needed to see how much of a mess I was (and am) to see how sweet God's gift of unearned favor really is. I mean, sure, I knew I needed grace. I can be selfish, I deserve far more speeding tickets than I've received, and my tongue could still use some major taming. But I thought I needed small grace, just enough to cover those minor transgressions. Subconsciously, I figured God was probably otherwise pretty pleased with me. (Holy arrogance, I know.)

Perhaps worse (for my soul anyway) than arrogance, the problem was, when I didn't feel as put together, I questioned if God did love me. Because somewhere along the line, my striving to "earn" love and acceptance became part of my relationship with God, too. I knew He loved other people who were far away from Him, but would He love me if I wasn't deserving of His love?

The answer is yes. In fact, that was kind of the whole point of Jesus dying on a cross to cover my sins and short-comings big and small. Turns out, we've all fallen short of the glory of God. And God loves us there.

Recall, Jesus hung on the cross (innocently) next to murderers who deserved the horrible death of crucifixion. With his last breath, one acknowledged Jesus as Lord and Jesus said that man could join Jesus in heaven. He hadn't changed his life to get into heaven. He hadn't made amends with those he'd wronged. He just knew he needed grace and believed Jesus could offer it. God's love covered the rest.

Perhaps more convicting for me, Jesus prayed for the mob who put Him on the cross. People who didn't even know they needed His forgiveness and grace. He prayed "Father, forgive them, for they know not what they do." While I'd like to think I wouldn't hang the Savior of the World on a tree to die, if I'm honest, my heart is probably more like the angry mob than the murderers on the tree. Because I often am oblivious to how much I need Jesus. I think I need minimal grace. I think I've probably "earned" most of God's love.

So, God gave me this precious season of utter brokenness to unlearn my idea of grace. To unhinge my pride and let me see clearly how much of a mess I was, and that His love would meet me right there, in the middle of my mess. But it didn't happen overnight. I would have to wade farther into the menacing waters of brokenness before I saw Him part the sea.

Chapter 6

Identifying the Pain

I was in pain. Serious pain. And judging from the depths of the pain, I knew it was about much more than my breakup with Sean. My breakup with Daniel wrecked me. But this was worse. So it had to be something deeper. I didn't immediately know what else was causing the pain, but knew I had to identify the pain so I could address it, and hopefully make it stop.

After a few months of Christine's wise counsel and God's mercy, I had clarity. My deepest pain points were my singleness and deeper feelings that I was unworthy and unlovable.

At this point in my faith journey, I knew God was God. Powerful, loving, able. But I didn't know how to expect, or even ask, for His best in a husband. I'd dated two men who I thought at the time were exactly what I wanted in a husband, and both left me. If these guys weren't it, then what else was out there? Honestly, I was afraid I'd have to settle. A solid, lasting relationship – someone choosing me and staying – it felt distant and unattainable.

I realized that I had spent years asking God questions about this area of my life. Why am I not adored? Where's extravagant love? I've got a lot of love to give - where's my male counterpart? With every new relationship, I thought I had found the answer. But every time a relationship ended, the questions resounded deeper. And then I would feel foolish. Foolish for dating a guy who abandoned me. Foolish for loving someone who could leave me. Foolish for investing so much time, energy, and love in men who weren't my forever mates.

In this deep pain of singleness, I realized that I actually felt more than foolish, I felt like a freak.

I was the common denominator after all, so I reasoned that something *I* was doing was incorrect, was unlovable. I thought I had plenty of self-confidence. But underneath, I had started to believe I wasn't lovable. How was love so easy and seamless for others and so difficult and elusive for me? What if I was cursed to be a spinster? I didn't know how to walk confidently when I felt unchosen in romantic relationships. Which caused shame. I felt undesired, discarded, "reserved for God" – all of which seemed like curses, not blessings. I looked around and started to feel like it was too late for me. Good Christian men got married at 25. As I re-read stories I'd previously found encouraging, I now found myself thinking 'you didn't go through it alone – you didn't live this hell of continued singleness.'

I almost started to expect God to say I'd be single forever since it is such a hard reality. My twisted view of God was that He was up in heaven saying, "let's make sure she's really all in and trusts me when I don't give her her greatest earthly desires." (Which, by the way, is a super twisted view of God and I'm glad Christine helped me unravel that toxic thought-pattern.)

These questions plagued me. They haunted me in the day and kept me from sleep at night. And I got low. Really low.

I felt really worthless. Really useless. Really unlovable.

No matter that I had just passed my second bar exam and was receiving high praise at my new law firm job. No matter that I had made it to Denver and was accomplishing my career ambitions. No matter that I had a cute apartment to live in and was surrounded by beautiful mountains to adventure in. No matter that I was "succeeding" by worldly standards on the outside. The pain, the feelings of unworthiness, and the lack of hope drowned out any gratitude I could muster for the rest of it.

I was depressed. And started wondering what the point of life was if I was destined to do it alone. Why not just get the misery over with? Outside of my family, who would really miss me? Besides, I loved Jesus so I was sure I'd go to heaven eventually – why not just start eternity sooner and get this pain over with? I lived on the sixth floor of my apartment building and had several moments of wondering what the real loss to the world would be if I simply jumped off my balcony?

You had suicidal ideations because of singleness? Yes, yes I did.

Depression isn't rational.

My mind had convinced me that if I couldn't get out of singleness, if this was my forever state, life wasn't worth living. I hated my singleness. And began to hate myself, to see myself as nothing. I didn't like me. And I didn't know why. I figured there must be something undesirable about me, some cause of my singleness, and if there was something so repulsive about me, so undesirable – maybe I was worthless.

I didn't want to feel that low. I didn't want to be depressed about my singleness. I just was. And it scared me. I had been slightly depressed before, but I had never gotten this low. I had never actually thought life might be better if it was over. I knew it wasn't right, but I couldn't shake the thought. Which made me more afraid, because now I once again couldn't control my own brain.

I can't tell you what snapped me out of it. I didn't have some magic "fix." I didn't "decide" life was lovely again. I certainly didn't logically "choose" to not be depressed. And I didn't "work" my way out of depression. My only contributions were that I kept going to counseling, kept taking my medicine, and kept praying (okay shouting) at God. But I know how depression works, and I can tell you, those three things alone are not always enough to battle Satan's lies. What I believe got me through this very dark season was that I had an army of prayer warriors around me who prayed the lies of hell away from me. And I am forever grateful for their petitions on my behalf. (Here's especially looking at you Mom, I know you prayed many tear-filled prayers for me in this season.)

Whether or not singleness causes you serious depression, as it did me, let's be honest about something – singleness is often hard. For those who got married at 21, you might be rolling your eyes and thinking, no Chelsea, marriage is hard. I have no doubt marriage is hard. But hear me out, singleness is hard after it's glamorous. And it often stops being glamorous after your mid-20s.

Singleness before then *is* glamorous – it's a career, it's freedom, it's adventure, it's travel, it's spending money however you want. But then it's redundant. Repetitive. Boring. Lonely. And hard. So, I want to make space for that here. Because for some of us, we haven't felt freedom to discuss that hard, and it's felt suffocating and lonely. So here is the freedom to call it out – singleness is hard.

But let's also be honest about depression – having dark thoughts doesn't mean you aren't a Christian. Battling lies of worth doesn't make you a freak. Depression isn't a sign of unbelief. Depression doesn't care how strong you are. It's not reserved for the "weak-minded" or "weak-willed." And Christians should be the last people to suggest as much.

Depression lies to us and isolates us. It tells us to be ashamed and afraid. It belittles us and tells us how stupid we are. And often, it makes us question our faith – like surely we wouldn't be this low if we really believed in God. I'm here to call BS. Faith is not immunity to depression. We live in broken bodies, and our brain chemicals can fail us just as much as our heart valves can. On top of that, we live in enemy-occupied territory.

Satan is alive and well. Since he can't destroy God (the war was won on the Cross), he's working like mad to destroy us, God's image-bearers. Satan is the father of all lies, and his best weapon is twisting good into evil. He often does this in our minds. Satan **LOVES** to get you alone and feeling lonely. Because he can lie to you about *why* you're lonely. He'll tell you it's because you're unlovable. Because you're a bad friend. Because you're horrible. Because you're ugly. Because you're fat. Okay, not fat, but too lumpy to be desirable. He'll tell you it's because you aren't enough. Or because you're too much. And in that vacuum of loneliness, you can start to believe it. That's where spirals can seriously happen, and where godly counselors are a literal godsend. If you've had those dark thoughts, you're not alone!

Again, for the people in the back: YOU ARE NOT ALONE.

Depression isn't a curse for those with little faith. Sometimes it's an attack from hell on those who will do the most damage to its cause. Many heroes of the faith battled depression – Martin Luther and Dietrich Bonhoeffer immediately come to mind.

I don't have a one-size-fits-all solution for depression. I don't even think licensed mental health professionals do. But I can offer a few suggestions from my own experience.

First, be honest! You need to get honest with yourself first. While it's scary to acknowledge how dark your thoughts are, you're going to be in a better position to fight them if you acknowledge them. You can't win against an enemy you're not fighting. You also need to be honest with someone you trust about what's happening in your head. Maybe it's a friend, maybe it's a pastor, maybe it's a counselor, but tell someone. I know that's scary. Especially if you consider yourself half as put-together as I used to. But I told Christine. And felt safer because someone knew.

Second, keep praying. (Shouts and breathless groans count too – read the Psalms.)

Third, be humble enough to get help. Maybe you need to ask for prayer. Maybe you need to get counseling. Maybe you need to go to the doctor and ask for an anti-depressant. In my case, it was all three. If only I were this lucky in Vegas! The anti-depressant had already been prescribed for my anxiety, but it took all three and that's okay.

Dark thoughts happen. Depression happens. But darkness has not overcome the world, and by the grace of God, it doesn't have to overcome you either.

Chapter 7

Be Careful What You Pray For

After I got through the darkest days, I realized I still needed more healing. While the suicidal ideations had ceased, my heart still felt sick. I needed healing. So I began to pray for God to heal me.

"I know You give space to mourn, to grieve, to question and to hurt. So heal me — not just from a broken heart but from the lies I believe about myself and Your love."

This is a dangerous prayer. And I didn't appreciate how dangerous it was at the time. I just knew I needed healing. Desperately. Most days this took the form of me begging God to heal me. Begging him to repair me, to heal my heart and change my toxic thoughts. To stop the tears. To fix my brain. To make my heart whole. While it didn't feel like it then, now I can see, He was answering my prayer, He **was** healing me. Even on those tear-filled days.

But can I be honest (and let you in on a secret if you don't already know)? Healing is painful.

Two months after my break-up with Sean, I penned these words:

"When does this get better? When does the pain stop? When do I see the end of this season? How does this get healed? And why am I so broken? And why must I be so aware of it? I need Your healing touch. I need my heart to believe what my head knows."

That particular season would continue for another five months. God still had things to reveal to me. When you ask God to show you Himself, He will. But He'll also necessarily have to show you the things you believe about Him that aren't true.

"Lord, I want to be whole, but it doesn't occur to me that You're a healer — You instead feel like a disconnected insurance provider, "covering" my healing but being far-removed, cold and unconcerned about my pain. Surely this isn't You. So show me You. Show me the God of goodness and fullness. Not a God of striving. Not a God of testing. Not a God of favorites, and the rest who must "earn" a seat at the table. Lord, be gentle with me. Be soft as I'm frail, weak, vulnerable and scared. I feel like an orphaned child wanting to receive the love of an adoptive parent, but unable to ignore the fear of abandonment and disappointment. Meet me here."

God had to root out lies I believed about my worth and my personhood, and lies I believed about His heart. I thought God was harsh. God had to give me slow, gentle healing to show me that

He's not. And I had to allow that healing process to happen every day of those painful, tear-filled five months.

But even gentle healing can hurt. Because wounds hurt. Even if you have just a slight cut, there's an initial sting. And most of us have experienced more than slight flesh wounds. The good news is, we were created for wholeness. So when God created our bodies, He gave us the ability to heal.

Actually, God designed our bodies with self-healing abilities. Think about the last time you nicked yourself shaving and a few weeks later, your skin was closed and healed — it's kind of wild when you stop and think about it. Our bodies know when something is wrong and get to work healing the wound.

When the wound is large or serious, modern medicine goes a long way in assisting the process. But deeper wounds often mean deeper pain in the healing process. As those who've been in a hospital bed know, sometimes you feel worse before you feel better. And sometimes the treatment and healing process feels downright unbearable.

When treating severe burns, doctors must consistently remove bandages and re-bandage the wounds. If they don't, the new skin can get infected. But removing bandages from partially burned, new delicate skin is a painful process. Excruciatingly painful according to the articles I've read by burn victims.

But it's the only way to heal.

And the doctors know this. So, they continue rebandaging, even while they see the pain on a patient's face, because they know that this is necessary to avoid infection. Because infection is often more deadly than the wound.

I think that's true in our spiritual lives as well.

Soul wounds left untreated become infected. And an infected soul affects everything in us and around us. God knows that, and desires to weed out everything that hinders us, including the toxicity of infection.

God doesn't do anything halfway. So when we ask for healing, He won't do anything less. The hard part of that is we often don't have the full picture of what needs healed. I thought my wounds were limited. But God saw more. And I'm now convinced He didn't settle on just what I thought needed healing because leaving the rest would have led to soul infection. To bitterness. To fear. To a life lived small.

This chapter is titled "be careful what you pray for" because when you pray for healing of your mind and soul, it might be painful. And I think we should be honest about it.

Healing hurts.

Asking for healing might expose fresh wounds, and old ones. Like getting bloodwork done or a CT scan, asking for healing might expose wounds and diseases you didn't even know were there. Things you'd learned to live with which, if left undetected and untreated for long enough, might kill you. Healing might tear off skin. It might cause extreme discomfort. It might hurt like hell. It honestly, at times, might feel like you're going to die.

But you won't. Healing is a process. And a process, by definition, has an end.

God can heal anything. And He can heal instantaneously if He chooses to. Think about the woman in the Bible who bled, or the blind man – both were instantly healed. Sometimes God does miraculously give immediate healing. But for most of us, healing is a bit more of a process. Sometimes a long process. Almost always a bit of a painful process. But our slow healing is no less of a miracle or prayer answered.

Praying for soul healing is a prayer that God loves to answer. I am confident that it's a prayer you'll see an answer to if you give God time to answer it. And allow Him to treat the wound. You might experience some discomfort (if not outright pain) while He does the healing work. But if you allow the healing, you'll be changed.

Part II

LIFE IS MESSY

Chapter 8

Accidental Lessons
from the Wrong Guy

I used to think God could only teach me good lessons when I was on the straight and narrow. I used to think God needed me to be right to show me Himself. I found out I was very wrong. As it turns out, He doesn't hide when I'm living in sin.

Some of the most important lessons I learned about sin, dating, love and delight – even God-designed love and delight – came from the wrong guy. A guy who wasn't even a Christian. A guy who was never supposed to be part of my romantic journey.

I had known him for a few years. We originally connected through mutual friends. I thought we were casual friends. He was in a different life season than me and wasn't a believer. The latter meant it was a no-go for me. While I found our conversations riveting – he was smart self-aware, cocky but caring (my favorite combination) – I never considered that might turn into attraction.

Now, before you judge me too much, thinking 'duh girl, you liked spending time with a man, of course you eventually like him, or at least consider if you like him,' I know – trust me, I know. I'm usually the one telling my girlfriends the same thing. I am well aware that sharing emotions and life with a member of the opposite sex often leads to 'feels.' It just sincerely was not on my radar with him.

Until a summer happy hour with a group of his friends, many of whom had become mine, on a rooftop patio with majestic views of the mountains. I started to notice he gave me special attention. His friends seemed to also notice. And maybe I was flirting with him, too? We all hung out for a few hours, and I was getting hungry. I told him I was going to head out to grab dinner and then head home. He insisted we should just get dinner together. I thought nothing of it as we got dinner together periodically (which I can't say I do regularly with men I'm interested in, let alone those I'm not, so apparently, I was just in la-la land on this one, but alas, I digress). I got ready to go – I was starving.

We left together, and as soon as we got in the elevator to leave the bar he leaned in – and kissed me. I was surprised. But it was a good kiss. So I kissed him back.

I wish I could tell you that we got dinner and then did things right and proper and he called me and asked me on a date. But I can't. Instead, we ended up back at his apartment. And kept kissing all night long.

That is not my usual M-O. And for the record, I want to clarify (more for his benefit than mine) that we did not have sex. But we walked right up to that line.

Why am I admitting this in a book about my journey into the heart of God? Because I'm human. And you're probably human, too. And I think the Church has done a bad job acknowledging sexual sin in a helpful way. The message is often just, "don't do it – it's a sin." Or the Church just ignores talking about it completely. Now I don't think we need to pander to the prurient (a nice law school word), but I personally wish more of the body of Christ (and those of us who have been oh, so blessed, by prolonged singleness) could talk honestly about the struggle. Because resisting sin in any form usually involves a struggle. While I'm very much in agreement that sex outside of marriage is a sin, the practical side of how to avoid it, and how to address the deep longings and desires it evokes seems to be lacking in popular Christian conversation. But I want it to be a part of the conversation the body of Christ is having.

I've wanted that for a long time. And in a fitful twist of irony, God tapped me on the shoulder and said hey, you could share about your journey. I've resisted (this is one of the last chapters of this book I wrote), but finally relented and said sure – let's use the girl who used to guard her image carefully, the one who thought she'd be a politician or Supreme Court justice and took great care to not misstep, and not be too public about anything. Sure God, why not this same girl to share her mess? (God has a sense of humor.)

So let me detour off of Alan for a bit (this guy's name is Alan by the way) to discuss why I think we need to be honest about sexual sin. I think we need to discuss it because it's such an easy sin to fall into.

It's enticing. It's fun. It sells the promise that it will validate us and make us feel worthy and beautiful. I think it's important to talk about sex because sex itself is not the problem. Sex outside of the way God intended it is the problem.

Everything God created is good. God created sex. So sex is good. Full stop.

But God designed it a certain way. A way that requires covenant love in a monogamous marriage between man and woman. Deep down, believers or not, I think we all know that. But we think we can ignore it. Satan's lie (which is amplified by our culture) is that we can get the good and great without doing it God's way. Satan tells us this **loudly** on the topic of sex. Unfortunately, Satan is a liar and the lie that we can enjoy sexual intimacy outside of covenant love is just that, a lie.

How do I know? Let's get back to Alan.

So, I spent the night at his place after the kiss I didn't see coming. I remember waking up and thinking "Chelsea Caroline, you should not be here." But that was not the moment I got up to leave. Faceplam. Not proud of that, but it's honest.

I knew I was wrong, intimate with a man I had no plan to marry, and my shame left me raw. Thankfully, I had an out. I'd taken an Uber to the happy hour the day before so I said I'd Uber home. Alan was a bit more emotionally aware than most guys I've known, and he sensed my shame (and new-found urgency to leave). Instead of letting me sit in it, he insisted I let him drive me home. I begged him to just let me Uber, but he didn't budge.

On the drive, he asked if he could take me to dinner that night, or some other time that week. I adamantly refused. I did not mince words telling him that while I had fun, it was a mistake and a one-time thing.

But Alan wasn't one to give up. Unbeknownst to me, his feelings for me had started before our elevator kiss. So, he was patient. He didn't push. He let me process my emotions and let me have distance for a few weeks. But, he also invited me back in. He told me we had great chemistry – that we connected at a deeper level. He told me how great I was. And reminded me how much fun we had together.

He told me it was normal to express attraction through intimacy. It was just part of our sexual natures. While my head knew that wasn't entirely true, my heart wanted it to be. He told me he knew I wasn't his future wife either – we disagreed on too many "big ticket" items – but why not explore this "connection" for a while? He told me I was amazing. That me, the real me (the one who had expressed her frustrations and insecurities and mess over dinners during a season of grief and depression when it hadn't registered with her that this guy might be into her) – that girl, who I saw as messy and unraveling, he saw as stunning and real.

Now, I know guys will tell you anything you want to hear to get you to go out with them. But being desired while I was vulnerable, messy and raw was new to me. I didn't know I could be lovely, even desired, when I wasn't "put-together." I didn't know being real could be beautiful. Don't get me wrong, I had plenty of unlovely, messy moments with prior boyfriends, but I was always **trying** to be presentable with them. I wanted to be the perfect girlfriend.

With Alan, I wasn't trying at all. I just was. And in his defense, he's a hopeless romantic who wasn't just trying to use me one time. He really did care for me.

I wrestled with this proposition. Dating Alan. Knowing I wouldn't marry him and our relationship wasn't building towards anything. I knew this path was not going to bring me my husband, and I knew I would get my heart broken, but I hadn't felt this 'spark' in a very long time. The Christian guys I'd interacted with in Denver after Sean were dull, or disgusting (if you say you're a Christian, how can you only be after sex?). So I accepted Alan's invitation to try whatever it was we had for a summer.

And about every two weeks I oscillated.

When we were together, I was high as a kite. We had fun going out to fancy dinners, putt-putting, watching sunsets over the mountains, grilling out and just being together. I was love drunk on our chemistry.

But when we were apart, this gnawing emptiness, shame, and regret would set in. Because I knew deep in my bones this wasn't God's design. I knew I was robbing myself, and Alan, of the true commitment that we were made for. I knew I was giving him too much and asking for too little. While he was valuing me and adoring me in every earthly way, it wasn't filling my soul. Because it was taking pieces of intimacy God designed for covenant love and trying to use it as a plaything.

When we were together, it was pure magnetism. I mean crazy attraction. So much so that a few times (yes – more than once) I went to dinner with the express intent of calling it quits and ended up kissing him instead and spending the night being held. So much for self-control.

I had nearly none with Alan. It's a good thing he respected me enough to want to respect my sexual boundaries because there were definitely times I otherwise wouldn't have. That was a God thing. This man had no qualms about having sex. At first, he was astounded that I wasn't going to engage and said we'd never work because of it. But something changed in him. While I know God didn't smile at my sin, I also firmly believe He protected me even in this season of it.

Years later, I can still say Alan is a good man. He's not a Christian and he's made some poor choices in life, but when I met him, he was one of the most emotionally healthy human beings I'd known to that point. He had gone to counseling. (Can I get an amen?) He had faced his past demons and asked for forgiveness from those he'd wronged. Quite frankly, he'd sought more healing in his life to that point than most of us Christians do in our lifetimes. Because of his emotional maturity, Alan was safe. And ridiculously patient. And fun. And a flirt with the best smile and a look that made me weak at the knees. And a good cheerleader. And I am convinced God held that.

We were off and on for a summer (because of my cycles of shame/delight, shame/delight as mentioned above). And then we were finally off. I finally pulled myself out of the addictive, intoxicating chemistry we had, knowing it was harming my soul more than it was doing good. While at first Alan asked me to reconsider, after I held my ground, he agreed with the decision as well. Which, honestly, was hard.

It had been so good for my feminine soul to be sought after and delighted in the way Alan did. It brought out my beauty and my confidence in who I was as a whole woman after a long season of feeling too broken, too complex, and too messy to be loved. I could be complex and still adored. I wasn't "too much." I found I was cherished and adored not because I was perfect, but because I could be lovely in my imperfection. I realized I didn't have to "earn" affection. It could be freely given. I found I was beautiful and worthy, without striving. I also found Alan becoming a better man, more tender, more servant-hearted, more humble, as we spent time together. And it was hard to give that all up.

There's a beautiful picture of Christ's love that happens in healthy marriage. Both see that they can be fully known and fully loved. Not loved once they're put together and "perfect." Loved as-is. And then changed because of that love. A picture of the Gospel.

God intended marriage to be a gift, a good gift, one that draws out the best in both man and woman. And I think dating relationships can bring out some of that, too. God made women to be delighted in. We reflect His beauty. As unique feminine image bearers, we were made to display beauty and reflect the delight that comes with drinking in something truly beautiful. And thank God he made men to enjoy our beauty in exactly that way. To be intoxicated by our femininity. But without the commitment of covenant love, that picture isn't as pretty.

I want to be as honest as I can here, because I want you to know these words aren't coming from someone who hasn't faced the struggle. I am very excited for sex in marriage. And in the long wait, I've crossed lines that my 21-year-old self would gasp in horror at. I am not perfect.

But I believe God, and He was very clear in telling us sex is reserved for marriage. Our culture would say no, that's incongruous

– you have desires so you must indulge, you must give in. Many in the Church would blush … or dismiss the reality of a desire for sex in unmarried singles, let alone single women. Surely if we were truly seeking Christ, the temptation would cease. (But that wasn't how it went for the apostle Paul, was it?)

I don't think either of those approaches work. The Bible is pretty clear that we are not to have even a "hint" of sexual immorality in us. Thanks be to God that He knew we couldn't live up to that and sent Jesus to cover our sinful ways, since heaven knows there's more than a "hint" of sexual immorality in me! (Hello, this chapter lays out a whole season of it!) I could go into the theology of why God calls us to righteousness and how His holiness can't be near sin, save for the blood of Christ, but I think that's what most of us already know, and if not, can readily hear in Church.

Instead, can I try to speak into that chasm which has too often been left by the Church on the topic of waiting for marriage to have sex? Mostly from learned experience and some earned wisdom along the way.

I really sincerely do believe that sex is a good gift that should be reserved for, and is best enjoyed in, a God-seeking, covenant-love marriage.

I also don't believe that God is out to steal my fun.

Here's what I know to be true, through my own choices and experiences, and listening to others who've had sexual experiences outside of marriage – as much fun as sexual intimacy can be, without the commitment, safety, and security of a covenant partner, that momentary ecstasy turns into insecurity, paranoia, fear, low self-esteem, and worse. Sex outside of marriage is never ultimately fulfilling, good or safe long-term for our feminine hearts. (It's not good for men either but this book isn't about them.) We've all heard somewhere along the lines that women aren't "good" at one-night-stands because they catch "feels." Instead of recognizing the God-given truth, and even protection behind that, we take it as an insult.

What if this is a piece of Satan's ploy to destroy us as women?

God created women to bear beauty to the world. To be lovely. To be welcoming and inviting. And yes, I think He created us to be sexy (read Song of Songs – desire is ***dripping*** off the pages). But in His design, He told us it was reserved. For marriage. And marriage was to be a reflection of His love for the Church, His bride. Satan's desire is to destroy the Church and destroy believers. He's called the "father of lies." And he will absolutely lie to us to get us to walk off a cliff and destroy ourselves. (Recall, Satan's first lie was to Eve – he's sought to destroy us since the beginning.)

Despite what our culture often tells us, sex wasn't meant to be transactional. Read that again. Sex was ***not*** meant to be transactional. It was not meant to "lure" a man in or "keep" him. It wasn't meant to be given to validate your beauty or worth. It wasn't meant to measure your likeability or sexuality. It wasn't intended to give you "power" or "control." ***Sex was not meant to attain***.

Sex was made to reflect. To reflect a woman's beauty. To reflect a man's strength and masculinity. To reflect love. To reflect safety. To reflect vulnerability and trust. To reflect wholeness. To reflect enjoyment. Good sex, biblical sex, reflects things that must already exist.

Sex does not determine a woman's beauty. Sex highlights it. Sex cannot create a good man. It can only reveal him. Sex does not create love or safety, but love and safety can create really good sex. The only place all of these things exist as a whole is in biblical marriage.

Can we circle back to where this chapter started? With Alan. I wish I was sitting next to you and we were swapping stories. You know how girls do? So just imagine we're having a cocktail at a cute bar or having coffee on a patio overlooking the mountains sharing stories. Hear me tell you that Alan **SHOWERED** me in affection – sweet notes, random texts throughout the day, flowers, head-to-toe kisses. He was the guy who held my hand whenever we were together, who took me on amazing dates, and lavished me in all he could offer. Alan represented the best this world has to offer. The best a relationship not centered on Jesus could be. *And it wasn't satisfying.* Because it wasn't God's design.

God's design is covenant love. Sex is good. But sex belongs in marriage. Sexual activity short of "sex" is still best reserved for marriage. I don't know where the line should be. I haven't perfected that in my own life. What I do know is this, outside of God's design of marriage, the fun, the excitement, the feelings of safety and even love – they go away. And then comes shame, insecurity and fear.

I am convinced that Satan has sunk his teeth into far too many women by selling us the lie that our worth, beauty, and even desirability will all be answered, affirmed, and assured through sex outside of marriage. Instead, he's rendered us insecure, crippled, and ashamed. He did so to me. And I don't want you to fall into the same trap I did.

So, can I end this chapter by telling you you're loved? You're lovely. You're beautiful and worthy whether a man has validated that for you or not. And you will never find that validation from sleeping with a man who isn't your husband. It will **NOT** be easy to withstand the temptation. But can you lean in with me and we'll both trust that it's worth it? That there's freedom in this choice? That God will indeed bless our obedience?

Chapter 9

Misadventures in Online Dating

*I*f I haven't made this clear, I really thought that I would easily meet someone as an adult in the "real world." (How blissfully naïve I was. Heavy sigh.) After Sean and I were over, I realized that I did not have a lot of places to meet people in said "real world."

Once Alan was off the table, I realized I knew almost zero single men in Denver.

So I went to the wonderful world of swiping, liking, commenting and chatting with perfect strangers online in hopes of finding Mr. Right. Denver was full of attractive men, so I was excited to quickly meet the love of my life. (Have I mentioned I'm impatient?) What I forgot is that online dating is emotionally exhausting if you're actually using it in hopes of finding someone. I've been told it's a numbers game, but if so, it's an exhausting one. The reality of online dating is that while yes, it can be thrilling, it can also be emotionally taxing.

Online dating for me typically falls into one of the following categories.

Option One:

I make a profile, swipe/like/heart some nice-looking strangers whose profiles indicate that they are Christian and have some modicum of intelligence or humor. I match with a nice stranger and we chat for about 48 hours before I realize they are "off" in some way. They are too forward (run away from guys who bring up sex within 24 hours), they don't ask any questions about me, they're already planning our future (before we've met), or some other "this doesn't feel right" characteristic pops out and I cut off that chat before it proceeds.

As I've found out, not all men who claim to carry the name of Jesus are safe men. Some are toxic. And it is **NOT** un-Christian to discern that and protect yourself. It's not "harsh" or "judgmental," it's wise. Trust me, dating one sociopath is enough for a lifetime (we'll get there).

Option Two:

I make a profile, swipe/like/heart some nice-looking strangers whose profiles indicate they are Christian and have some modicum of intelligence or humor. I match with a nice stranger and we chat for a few days, or sometimes weeks without much excitement. We decide to meet up anyway, and the date is every bit as anti-climactic as the chatting has been and we usually both say some niceties about how we should do this again, but neither of us ever follows up – at all. (While I'm very against ghosting people, I consider this option to be acceptable. I'd like a man who pursues me and at the very least txts me after a date. If he doesn't txt me, I see no need to txt him, especially in this situation, where it was pretty clear we are not going to become each other's better halve). I don't think Christian + Christian is the only requirement to a good relationship. God created us uniquely, so while I don't necessarily think there is one perfect guy out there for me and anyone else would be a waste of my time, I do think God is personal, creative, and unique, and there are probably only a handful of men well-suited for me, and me, for them. I digress.

Option Three:

I make a profile, swipe/like/heart some nice-looking strangers whose profiles indicate they are Christian and have some modicum of intelligence or humor. I match with a nice stranger and we chat for a few days or weeks and we have good conversation. Typically he will ask me to dinner or coffee or drinks, and I enthusiastically say yes (although there have been a few times where I couldn't wait for him to ask and I asked to meet up). We meet and have a great time. We laugh, we smile (I think he's super cute), we find out we agree on a variety of topics, and we have a great date.

Another Sidebar: Dating for me is a vehicle to finding a partner in life who is also chasing Jesus, and will do so by my side. That is a non-negotiable for me, so I do not spend time and emotional energy on someone who does not fit that bill. (Been there, endured that heartbreak, learned the lesson.) Second, I see politics as a lens into your worldview. I understand that Christians come in all sorts of political preferences, but I want to partner with someone whose worldview aligns with mine. Not because I think people who disagree with mine are evil. But because I want to build a life with someone. If we don't share our worldview, we're entering discord and disagreement from the jump. No thank you. Also, I should point out that nearly every modern dating site or app allows you to identify what religion you are and what your political leanings are so it's something you can pretty much filter out before you even match with someone. And if you know you agree, it's more fun to launch into conversation about everything because you don't have to side-step everything that could be considered controversial in this crazy world.

Which brings me back to **Option Three**. We have a great first date. We are both enthusiastic about a second. The second date happens in short order, and we have a great time again. I'm excited.

> *"Thank You for a great date, Lord. I'm hesitant to be excited already, but he's cute (okay he's hot), he's responsible, he wants a wife and children and he has planned for that. He's sweet and strong. He likes my brain (and my butt), and he seems to really love You. Thank You."*

And just as things are getting good, they start to derail. We might make it to a third, fourth, or even fifth date before this man falls off the face of the planet, but at some point, he ghosts me. Or, equally confusing, keeps talking to me in random intervals, but never makes a plan to get together again. I'm left confused, and often crushed.

This letdown is Satan's playground to mess with my mind. If you didn't know this, ghosting is actually bad for your brain.

"There's a profound lack of closure to the relationship, an ambiguity that makes it impossible to interpret what went wrong. You may think your partner has begun dating someone else — or, worse, that they've finally recognized the things you hate about yourself. Ghosting causes you to question yourself ... [and] deprives you of any chance to work through what went wrong in the relationship. In other words, it's altogether too easy to draw troubling conclusions when you've been ghosted."

Yes! For anyone who has been ghosted, you know this is all true. You question what is so wrong with you that someone just deserted you. You question if you're not pretty enough or smart enough, or too smart or too opinionated. You question if you're worthy of love and affection.

Even if you know that ghosting isn't a reflection on you, the lack of closure is well, lacking. And if you didn't know that, hear this loudly – GHOSTING IS NOT A REFLECTION OF YOU. It is entirely about the other person. I realize this isn't always comforting. It hasn't been for me. But I find dealing with the world, and my circumstances through the lens of reality and Truth is always the first step in the right direction.

Option Four:
I make a profile and am immediately underwhelmed by the prospects. Let me back up. If you haven't been on a dating app lately, I'll let you in on what becomes a pretty obvious secret – the algorithms of most are set up to show you the most impressive, beautiful people first. Usually your first day on the app is exhilarating. There's the handsome doctor who flies prop-planes as a hobby, the gym owner who is F-I-T, the pilot who rescues puppies,

the firefighter who has a big family, the business owner who has traveled the world, the veteran who served 10 tours and is getting his MBA. The possibilities are endless! With so many interesting attractive men out there, surely I'll find my husband! Perhaps I have too much confidence, but I assume I could match with any of these men. (I just assume that they're looking for a smart, sweet, curvy Christian woman with a good head on her shoulders and plenty of sass … I am, apparently, mistaken.) In all of my (unfortunately long) history of online dating I have matched with exactly zero of these initial prospects. (I am half convinced the dating apps make them up.)

So, knowing this is how dating app algorithms are typically set up, if you make a new profile and not only do not see these stellar candidates, but see a bunch of "bleh," it's underwhelming and disappointing. "Bleh" is a lot like "blah" but I think worse. The dictionary definition of "blah," is "dull or unexciting." Bleh is blah on steroids. And it actually causes me anxiety. It makes me feel like I've missed the boat.

> *"Online dating has become my own form of hell — trying to find one in a million, staying hopeful while getting repeatedly passed over. I know I'm not better and we're all sinners and You love us all but honestly, this feels like bottom-feeding. Men who can't make a plan, who are offended by making the first move. Men who want easy — in every sense of the word. Where's a real man — who can and will face hard things?"*

Option Four is feeding ground for Satan's lie that all the good ones are taken and I'm left dumpster-diving through a reject pile.

I realize that this is not objectively true and there are good men out there. But I also know a lot of women in my shoes feel this way, and someone needs to just be honest enough to say this is how we too often feel. Is it a lie from Satan? Yes. But does it feel overwhelmingly real in the moment? Also yes.

The older you get on a dating app, the older you feel. I met Sean on Tinder at 26 (don't judge – it was Nebraska and wasn't what it is today). I've still had to dabble on dating sites in my 30s and let me tell you it feels different. Suddenly the prospects went from thrilling, exciting, about-to-take-on-the-world men to divorcees and fathers, and sometimes just some weirdos. God has redemptive stories, but as women, this isn't what we dreamed of as little girls. Divorce and remarriage involve brokenness, and often sin. It's not Plan A of God's design for marriage and children. He can ***absolutely*** redeem it – I've seen it in close friends' lives! But it can also create a weird headspace for those of us who are still searching for our future husbands.

It can start to feel like I don't deserve good, let alone great. I begin just wondering if there's someone out there who will like me after a first date, will call for a second (or txt – I'm not even picky anymore), let alone someone who has the fortitude, character, and stability to be a husband or father. And a leader in a dark world. Then add being a husband to a strong, opinionated, fierce, highly-educated female and I feel like all of these qualities I want to love about myself are actually somehow cons in dating. That they mean I won't find someone. That they aren't valued by today's standards, sadly, at times, even within the Church.

Another side-bar. MEN WHO PUT "CHRISTIAN" ON THEIR PROFILE AND ALSO ADD THAT THEY'RE ONLY LOOKING FOR "SOMETHING CASUAL"? SO YOU JUST WANT SEX, BUT WANT SEX FROM A "CHRISTIAN" GIRL? I HONESTLY WANT TO PUNCH YOU IN THE GROIN. GET OUT OF HERE WITH THAT NONSENSE!

Here's the other thing about online dating, it's not set up to help you correctly assign value to humans. It's very much window shopping. And mostly visual. Even for us ladies who apparently don't care as much about appearance as our male counterparts.

You also know that you're not exclusive with anyone from the jump. Like this isn't a rom-com where a guy saw you in the supermarket and was mesmerized by you and asked you out, nor someone you know who finally gets the nerve to ask you out. And seeks to pursue JUST you. No, online dating means, at any given time, he is talking to just as many people as you are. That he has multiple dates a week. The gentlemen don't mention this. But really, what a low bar.

I'm not saying dating apps are bad, because they're not. But they can be really depressing, and even, at times, tools of hell to discourage, cripple and derail women from the goodness of romance that is part of God's design. I don't have answers. I'm writing this 100% single, so I can't tell you a magic formula to find the right guys. I just have experience, and a feeling that I'm not alone. And since my desert involves my singleness, it just felt like a subject begging to be voiced.

Many of you will find your spouses through a dating app. It's the world we live in. But it's okay if sometimes they suck. It's okay if you need to take a break from them to stop the incessant feeling of paranoia that if you don't check this app every 5 hours you might miss your Mr. Right. It's also okay to have boundaries and standards. To know what you're looking for. I'm not saying God will honor a grocery-list of shallowness, but I think He'll honor hearts that desire what He wants – godly leadership, servant-heartedness, attraction, enjoyment of the other, shared vision and values.

And when you have some sucky dates or experiences, just know you're so not alone. It's rough out there. Keep your chin up. And guard your self-worth and sanity in the process of swiping/hearting/liking and dating.

Chapter 10

When You Encounter Toxic Men

*A*s I've already mentioned, I had an unhealthy expectation for much of my life, that if I did the right things, I'd get the right thing. Which, even after a lot of counseling and prayer, still carried into my dating life. I knew there was no "perfect" person out there and my prayers had changed to asking for my "imperfectly-perfect-for-me" partner. At 29, I was much healthier – having loved and learned through several serious relationships and ensuing breakups, through forays into non-Christian relationships, and lots of Godly counseling – figuring out who I was and how to embrace that woman. So I really thought dating at this point would be easier.

It was not.

Not seeing any prospects appear anywhere naturally, I had hastily made a profile on yet another dating app after dinner with a good girlfriend. I recall complaining to God, "I am super thankful for all the absolutely incredible women You've placed in my life in this season, but how is it even statistically possible that I don't know one, not one, eligible Christian man?"

To set the scene of this tantrum (one of many around this subject), I was in a co-ed bible study at the time, which had been a great place of growth, safety and community. While I was very thankful for that community, it was pretty clear this was not going to be the place where I found a spouse.

Yes, there were men in the group. But less than a handful were single. And frankly, the only thing I had in common with any of the single men in that group was that we loved Jesus, lived in Denver, and were in this bible study. Which, in case you're wondering, is not enough to check the box of "life partner" or "soulmate."

On that note, can I take a moment to get into what I believe is one of the most unhelpful things that some in the Church have come to believe and teach?

Let me preface by reiterating that I am 100% in agreement with what God says about marriage. Namely, that it's a reflective picture of Christ's love for his bride, the Church and the relationship of God with Himself – God, Jesus and the Holy Spirit – having holy communion within Himself. That it's to be between a man and woman, each uniquely bearing characteristics of God. That it is to display the beauty and wonder of a relational God. That, even for a strong woman like myself, the husband is to be the leader and the wife is to submit – under the love of a man who sacrificially loves her like Christ. I am in firm agreement with all of that. It's what I'm still praying for and seeking.

So why is it that the Church often tells single Christians that there's a simple formula for "Christian" marriage: 1 Christian + 1 Christian = good Christian marriage?

As a female over 30, I have entertained this question *A LOT*. I have wrestled with it, prayed about it, sought lots of godly counseling and advice on it, and what I've arrived at is this – that's a BS formula. You read that correctly, it's horse manure.

Here's my view: if a Christian marriage is to mirror Christ's love for the Church, then it should be something beautiful, personal, intentional, and delightful. God made me uniquely. The Bible is clear that He has certain plans and thoughts about me. He made you uniquely. We both display His handiwork, but in different ways. He didn't make us all lawyers (thank goodness). He didn't make us all artists. He didn't make us all brunette. He didn't make us all 5'8". He didn't make us all first children or extroverts. He's creative.

If we have such a personal, creative God, why in the world would we think that who we get married to isn't deeply personal, creative, and planned?

I won't go so far as to say I think there is one and only one person for each of us. But I do seriously think God cares about our hearts, our lives, and our missions. And I don't think just any fellow believer would make a good partner for me, or me for them.

To my fellow singles who have felt belittled by fellow Christians who have told you that you're too picky because you won't date or marry just any single Christian man that they throw in front of you, I'm sorry. There's a serious difference between unhealthy expectations (he has to be 6 feet tall and have so and so profession and be a middle child and make more money than I do and have been a college athlete with a heart of gold) and having God-given desires, hopes, and yes, even standards, for a marriage (he needs to be walking with Jesus, in community with other Christian men, seeking purity, and learning humble leadership). The latter are **healthy**.

Anyway, living in Denver, I didn't meet a whole lot of Christians in "real life." And meeting a Christian man was feeling more and more difficult (if not impossible). But after a few days on this dating app, I matched with a *STUD*.

I couldn't believe we matched. He wasn't just seriously attractive, he was a Christian girl's dream man (I thought he was mine anyway). He was a bartender turned firefighter turned nerdy middle school science teacher whose hobbies were astronomy and hockey. Chase was charming, intelligent, enthusiastic, and seemed very self-aware.

He was older than me, a divorced dad of two beautiful preteen daughters. Although marrying into an instant family wasn't exactly the dream, I was recently open to the idea.

We moved our first date up from Sunday to Saturday because he decided he couldn't wait to meet me. Due to our schedules, breakfast was the only time we could meet but I was pretty excited about him, too, so breakfast it was.

When I saw him walk out of his Jeep I was heart-eye-emoji. And he immediately gave me that look – you know the one – that told me he felt the same way about me. We sat down and started to chat and ordered breakfast. And conversation just flowed. We jumped in - talking about Jesus, about life, about his girls.

We had talked for three hours before we both reluctantly realized we couldn't sit at this restaurant and talk forever. He walked me to my car and we pretended to talk for a second and then he leaned in for a kiss. A great first kiss. So great that we had to have a second, right there in the parking lot.

I didn't know until that moment that he hadn't kissed anyone since his divorce, and was baffled when he said "well dang, that's what I've been missing for three years, hopefully you thought that was as good as I did." Chase had been divorced for three years, and had just recently entered the dating world at the suggestion of a co-worker. He'd spent the last three years healing from the divorce (including going to counseling) and focusing on his girls. Swoon.

We parted ways and I drove home. I was trying to play it cool (because we still had another date the next day – our originally scheduled first date that we both eagerly wanted to keep as a second date). But this man had no chill. He txt me like immediately. And was bold enough to say "hey, I really hope that was your last first date." UM WHAT? Usually, I would think that's crazy. Way too soon. Way too bold. But I felt the same way. I played it a bit more cool, but barely.

Our second date was just as amazing. While we were both dressed pretty casually on our first date (it was breakfast after all), this man showed up for lunch Sunday in a blazer and jeans and I think I was weak at the knees. (Look, I'm not blind, and I think God created men and women to enjoy each other, and I am not ashamed of that.) We had another great date, and we were close to my house, so I invited him to come over and hang out after lunch.

We chatted and hung out for a while, but the chemistry was intense, and we had a pretty steamy make-out session on my couch. And then, without my prompting, Chase informed me that we needed to talk about boundaries.

What? A man who leads on this most uncomfortable, unfun conversation? How could this man get better?

I actually wanted more relaxed boundaries than he did, even though I was committed to saving sex for marriage. But after hearing his heart, hearing his desire to build something lasting, and not let lust guide us, I knew he was right and was trying to lead in a Christ-like way. So, we decided on pretty strict boundaries, at least from my standpoint. Nothing more than kissing. On the mouth. Ever. No beds. No sleepovers. Not even a nap together. And nothing that would lead us to that sort of temptation. I was floored by his leadership on this subject.

With every subsequent date, he seemed to get better. We were dating on Valentine's Day, but he had the girls and had promised to do a father-daughter date with them. I was a bit bummed, but tried to put on a good face. He had a crazy week that week and I knew he was stressed, so I kept my feelings side-lined, knowing he'd make it up to me later. But he knew I was bummed and without my asking or prompting, sent two dozen beautiful red roses to my office on Valentine's Day.

I'll be honest, usually this would annoy me, but everything he did felt special, and I was actually accepting this man's affection rather than pushing him away.

He was great. And I was starting to fall. Hard. I really could see how he might be the right man for me. I was starting to ask God how to prepare for step-motherhood. I was excited about building something for the Kingdom with this man.

I know that's way too soon. I thought so then. But I thought there was something good, even holy, between us, so I tried to be open to the possibility.

We had had our first real 'fight' on a Sunday about a month and a half into dating. It was something about how I thought it was unfair he was always asking me to trust him as he was already planning our life together but hadn't brought me into the real parts of his life. Yes, after 40ish days of dating, Chase was convinced we were going to get married and already spoke often of such things. He was planning where we would live (he taught on the south side and I lived downtown), how we would minister together, and more.

I was torn. Part of me was flattered that this man seemed to really see me and cherish who I was as a woman and be eager for the chance to marry me. After all, I rationalized, I am pretty great, and I've been waiting for a man who saw how great I am to jump on the opportunity to do life with me. But, some of Chase's words didn't match his actions. He was a dad, after all. And while he was eagerly planning our nuptials, I hadn't met his daughters, or his family (who were local). I was not in a rush to be introduced to family or children, but since he was in a rush with everything else, this lack of interaction seemed incongruous.

I said as much to Chase and he got a look on his face I'll never forget. It was someone else. It was cold and cruel.

He told me I was crazy to think I should meet his daughters so soon. I told him it wasn't that I wanted to, it's just that if he wasn't ready for that, we needed to slow down on the talk of the future, because a lot of things needed to happen before then. But he wasn't hearing it.

I've had plenty of disagreements with boyfriends before, but this one was odd. He was more than distant. I didn't feel we had resolved anything, but something told me he wasn't going to budge to resolution or talk through things so we hung out for a bit and then I left soon after.

And a few days later, I'd learn, he was done. Bliss ended as fast as it started.

The man I had dated exclusively, who had professed his desire to marry me on date 3 – he was gone. He just out of the blue stopped responding to my texts and didn't call me (he had called me every day since our first date).

I was completely confused. Honestly, I was rattled.

While I didn't totally trust Chase, I thought we were building towards trust. He said he wanted to build towards forever. We did church together. He prayed for me. We were dreaming about how we could impact God's kingdom together. But then he summarily dumped me? Not even dumped, ghosted me.

I was spinning. I couldn't make sense of it. A week after he stopped responding to me, I took the weekend to try to find some clarity and re-center.

That Saturday, he txt me. And told me I was crazy and to please never talk to him again. If I was shaken before, I was nearly trembling then.

Until clarity hit like a ton of bricks – something was off, and it wasn't because of me. I don't know where this knowledge came from, but something in my spirit knew that this ghosting was not normal and wasn't my fault, but that I had dated a very toxic man.

I don't know where this knowledge came from, I wasn't familiar with the characteristics of a sociopath, nor was it a term common in my vocabulary. But something in my spirit knew that was my answer.

I immediately googled 'characteristics of a sociopath'. "Lies, deceives and uses others for personal gain." "Shows aggressive or aggravated behavior." "Doesn't feel guilt or remorse." "Uses humor, charisma and charm to manipulate others." "Has a sense of superiority and strong, unwavering opinions." "Not able to keep positive friends or relationships." "Being cold."

Wait a minute – all of these described Chase.

I had started to see that some things were off around the time we broke up. He had a seriously inflated ego – he repeatedly told me he thought he was better than everyone else, but would try to flatter me and tell me he thought I was better than him. I'm not crazy – a man who honestly believes he's better than everyone else is a problem.

He didn't have close friends despite being in the area for years. And he had many strained relationships.

He blamed his ex-wife entirely for their divorce, saying she was a narcissist. He was a victim. This obviously tugged at my heart-strings, but looking back, I question the sincerity of this story.

He would lie about small things. He was sweet to me at first, but then, if he didn't get exactly what he wanted when he wanted, he would get aggressive, or cold. He started to tell me how I would respond to certain future things. Like what I'd say upon meeting his mom, or going to the lake with his family. At first I thought it was sweet – I thought he was showing that he knew me, and saw me.

But post-breakup I realized they weren't responses I would have. He wasn't telling me he knew me, he was priming me for the expected behavior he wanted from me. It was creepy and terrifying to realize I had spent time with someone who was so manipulative.

I remember going to counseling and telling Christine everything that happened, and that I thought Chase was a sociopath. She agreed – she said my description led her to the same conclusion.

How, I asked? How did I end up dating a crazy person? A toxic person? I was healthy. I felt whole for the first time in a long time. How did that happen? Was everything upside down? Was I unable to discern a good man? Was I looking for something wrong? Or worse, evil?

Christine assured me that no, I wasn't unable to discern a good man, and I shouldn't feel bad. Professionals can't diagnose sociopaths until they've had several sessions with one. And instead of keeping him around, she said, I scared him off. Apparently, sociopaths don't scare easily. They sink their claws in. And hang on. They wreak havoc on their prey.

I was lucky, she said. Protected, actually. She had never seen a sociopath voluntarily retreat. Let alone run away. But Chase did. In fairly short order.

I'd like to say that was immediately comforting, but it wasn't. I was rattled for months afterward. Conveniently, we broke up a few weeks before the world shut down for COVID which both brought clarity and made it worse. The clarity was gratitude that I wasn't dating a terribly toxic person in the middle of my first global pandemic. As no one did well during 2020, I became more and more grateful that I was not left to find out how much more toxic this man got during a time that was crazy for everyone.

But COVID also gave me time to sit with my anger and disappointment and confusion. I was angry God allowed a really broken man into my life. I was angry at how Chase broke my trust − my ability to trust men, and my ability to trust my gut. I was angry that I had thought Chase was so good − angry that I had started to ask God to make my heart ready to be a good wife to him and a good step-mom to his daughters.

I asked God hard questions. *"Is everything I desire evil?"* *"Is everything I hope for a lie?"* *"Are my longings so misplaced that they lead me to trauma?"*

And perhaps the one that echoes in the background of my story for the past decade − *"why have You allowed this?"*

It's been over three years since Chase traumatized my understanding of romance and men. I can't say I understand why God allowed it. At the time, I really thought Chase was a hand-picked special delivery from the heavenly realms. I really was prepared to enter into an instant family, and the hardships of step-mother-hood. I knew marriage would look different than I expected, but I was ready for the unexpected.

I'm still not thankful for Chase, but I am thankful that I was quickly released from his snare. I'm thankful for Christine's wise counsel and realizing I didn't do anything wrong to deserve Chase's lies and abandonment. I'm thankful, now, that he did ghost me. That my belief in his delusions ended quickly. I feel protected in that way.

While I wouldn't wish it on anyone, I am also thankful that I now know how to spot a dangerous man. One of my best friends dated one, too. And getting to talk with her about the psychological traumas we endured from these men was freeing. I wasn't alone. And neither was she. Bad men happen to good women. While I was lucky to get dumped so quickly, most toxic men keep their victims ensnared for a long time. For my best friend, it was years.

At this point in time, I think God allowed Satan that room so that I could tell you, if you've experienced a toxic man, you're not alone. Unfortunately, there are some bad men out there. And sometimes they prey on really good women. I'm convinced it's a scheme of hell. While it took time for me to regain trust in myself, in men, and even in God, I can now see that Satan intended destruction for me – if he couldn't get me stuck in a bad relationship, his next step was convincing me to lose trust in all men.

And I did, for a while. But one toxic man does not make the whole batch bad. Even though I've experienced a bad man, not all men are bad. There are still safe, good, godly men out there. They are rare gems – trust me, I know – but they're out there. Having had a bad man play a role in your life does not preempt a good one yet to come.

I'm still not sure why God allows all of what He does, but I do know that the evil of this world doesn't have to destroy you. Or your hope. Or your trust in all men. Or all people. And it doesn't mean you deserved what happened to you. That you weren't smart enough to avoid the pain. That you were too dumb, or naïve, to avoid this evil. As anyone with a brain knows, bad things happen to good people. Sometimes bad men happen to good women. I don't have an explanation for it, but I'll hold space to let you know you're not alone if you're one of those women. And I'll remind you that God is still writing the rest of your story.

Chapter 11

Acknowledging Trauma

I have experience with trauma. (An anxiety attack on an Indiana interstate, my Fourth of July with Daniel, dating Chase, and more.) But I'm pretty sure it's not just me. I'm 99.9% certain we have all experienced trauma.

Some of you might be thinking, "no, not me. Life is good and God is good, and 'trauma' is something others have experienced." Others of you are reading this thinking "thank God someone else can relate."

I am not a professional, so I do not have any background in the psychology of trauma outside of a Psych 101 class I took in undergrad (which I didn't ace). This chapter isn't for that. There are tons of awesome resources for that and I'm happy to point you to them. But that's not what I'm offering in this space.

I'm offering what I have. Experience.

A place to acknowledge trauma, or maybe start to. A place to hopefully be encouraged to work through it. Because stuffing it actually eats us alive.

While "trauma" is often a red-flag word, at its core, trauma means a deeply distressing or disturbing experience. Being a human for any length of time means experiencing something distressing or disturbing at some point along the road. If you are reading this book and lived through 2020, I can say with 100% certainty that you, my dear, have indeed experienced trauma.

Outside of 2020, our traumas are wide-ranging. Some of us had horrific home lives as children. Others experienced awful accidents that took loved ones too soon. Others have suffered alongside a loved one's illness. Others have been the one in the hospital, or with the diagnosis of a debilitating mental illness. Some have been victims of abuse, others victims of assault, and still others have been scarred by relational wounds. And I'm sure that list isn't all-inclusive.

We live in a culture that wants to tell us if we've experience trauma, we're victims, and that we should identify loudly in that victimhood. While there are plenty of traumas to which we were victims, I've found for my own traumas, victimhood doesn't provide a good path to healing.

Instead, acknowledging trauma and working through it does. As much as I'd like to, I can't undo what's happened to me or been done to me. I can't erase it.

But I have to acknowledge that trauma has changed me.

In my head I categorize trauma as different than a "wound." Or at least, it follows square-rectangle logic. A square is a rectangle, but a rectangle isn't a square. Trauma is a wound, but not all wounds are trauma – because trauma changes everything. A wound is getting a scrape on your knee. Trauma is losing your entire limb. It doesn't heal the same way. Losing a limb will fundamentally change your life.

That's what trauma does. It changes your life.

It changes your brain. It changes your thoughts. It changes your heart. It can change your relationships. It changes stuff. And the change is never good. At least, not initially. The change trauma brings is chaotic and messy. It's broken and dark.

So, we have to address it. Because until we do, we're ignoring the elephant in the room. We're ignoring how trauma changed us for the worse.

The only way out of trauma in my life has been through it.

Trauma has taken different shapes in my life, and often, I've tried to "logic" my way out of it. I try to tell myself it wasn't as bad as something else that could've happened. Or that I probably somehow brought it on myself. Or that it really wasn't even that bad at all and I should just get over it. (God bless Christine for helping me see these (toxic) thought-patterns.)

Sometimes, I honestly just didn't know I had trauma. And sometimes, I knew I had trauma, but I didn't know what to do with it. I'm not one to stick my head in the sand and avoid things. For better or worse, if I see a problem, I address it. And this is especially true in my own brain and thought patterns. I am *very* eager to get out of the mess. Even if it's within my own skull.

Christine has helped me see that sometimes I need to get through it, not out of it. Maybe that's a distinction without a difference, but it feels different. I want to get out of trauma quickly. **VERY** quickly. I want it to go away. So, I'd rather run away from it (even if I'm not really healed) than walk through the process of acknowledging it and working **through** it.

But **through** is the only path **out**. There are different ways "through" depending on what your trauma was and how your brain works and who you are. If you haven't picked up on my not-so-subtle plug for Christian counseling yet, here's an explicit plug – get yourself a godly Christian counselor! Because they have knowledge and wisdom that I don't. They know how our brains work. And how we can heal them.

It turns out, our brains are crazy resilient. We can actually build new neuropathways. We can heal – even from the worst traumas. Our brain can rebuild in similar ways to how our skin can regrow after burns. But it takes work.

All I have is "from now on." At a certain point, my trauma can't be my excuse for my life, I must own this one precious life I've been given.

Please hear that with a tender grace. I am so NOT minimizing the pain of your trauma! If I had found solace in sitting in mine and playing the victim card, I'd be the first to tell you to do the same. But that path only leads to bitterness, fear and anger.

So, I've had to choose to acknowledge and address trauma. No matter how horrible the trauma was (or will be – I'm 32, I'm sure there's more to come), I do get to choose how to approach "from now on." Please hear me clearly, because I do not in any way intend for that to be callous or cold. I'm not saying it from a place of judgment. I'm actually speaking from freedom. From a place where I'm no longer enslaved to the trauma or the perpetrator thereof, I'm free to live again.

While there are still things I can't fathom healing from (being sold into sex slavery as a child usually tops this list in my mind), God says He can heal even that. And I've seen Him heal some really broken stuff in my life.

But let's be honest about what He doesn't say – He doesn't say it never happened. He doesn't say the memories are wiped. He doesn't say we get some kind of heavenly amnesia and forget the traumas. No, in heavenly math that I don't understand 1 horror + 1 God can yet result in good.

And I don't know how that works or when it happens. I think often it doesn't fully happen on this side of eternity. And I still can't fully wrap my head around that either. But I'm slowly starting to lean into it. To see His timing is long. And He cares about the hurts in my heart and life. And will walk with me as I walk through the healing process. He'll walk with you, too. So will I. (And final plug, so will a good counselor!)

Chapter 12

Talking About Trauma

I had another traumatic experience recently that made me realize that while acknowledging and working through trauma is *so* important to our mental, emotional and spiritual health, I truly believe there's also freedom and Kingdom power when we talk about it with our sisters.

I believe that so much, in fact, that I added this chapter after I thought this book was done. I was so convinced it included everything God wanted me to say that it had already gone through lots of loving eyes being edited and prayed over. (And getting revised by women who are far better at grammar than I am.) I thought the writing part was done. And if I'm honest, I hoped the messy stuff was in the past.

But God had other plans. A night I didn't see coming took my breath away. Soon after, it made me realize maybe we need to talk more about trauma here.

I have a few major caveats before we get into this chapter. Let's state what should be obvious but sometimes isn't – not everyone is safe. Nothing in this chapter is advocating sharing your hard stuff with just anyone. I am not, nor ever will be someone who thinks it is appropriate or wise to air every messy thing in your life to everyone, via social media or otherwise. Honestly, even some of your closest friends and family won't always be safe for every broken thing in your life. There is wisdom in knowing who to share with and when. And I pray God gives you that wisdom as you read these words. With that caveat, let's talk more about trauma.

As I drove away from this latest knockout that left me feeling like I had just had my teeth kicked in, I knew I needed to talk about it. Immediately! So I called Christine. And I'm not usually that client! Christine could tell you that I've actually been through worse and waited for months to talk to her while she was on maternity leave. (Which hindsight says was stubborn pride, and was definitely a mistake, but I digress.)

This night, this time, I knew I would spiral quickly if I didn't run the situation by someone who knew me, knew about the people involved, and could speak Truth into it. And thank goodness, Christine picked up. And talked me down for the night in a period of about ten minutes. And had space for me to have a full session the next day to further process what happened.

Because I was a nervous wreck. I felt like I'd had the wind knocked out of me. I was completely discombobulated. (The technical term is "unregulated.") And I had a day of *feeling* that. My nervous system was shot. My soul felt fatigued. And I was angry/confused/hurt/mad/sad/depressed in a constant rotation every half hour. But I've now had enough counseling to recognize when my nervous system is taking over, and knew I'd have to ride the wave until it passed.

So, I sat in the weight of my feelings, with my nervous system taking over, but I didn't let it overtake me. I didn't have the energy to go to the gym, so I took a hot bath. I gave myself a hug (seriously, it's good for your nervous system). I got a manicure and pedicure knowing touch also soothes the nervous system. I went to the park and read a book. Then had a counseling session. And by the time my head hit the pillow that night, within a span of 24 hours, I realized I could face this trauma. This time, I knew I'd get back up swinging. Maybe not the next day. Maybe not for a while, but I would get back up.

So, talking about trauma is important first because if we can talk about it real time in a safe place – if we can share it real time, we can address it and face it. We can avoid getting sucked into the wormhole that Satan intends for us with whatever trauma he throws our ways. That wormhole has a name. It can come out a lot of different ways, but somewhere, there's usually shame.

I find that I often feel ashamed that trauma happened to me. I feel ashamed that a not-ok situation befell me. I feel like a fool that it happened – was it my fault? I start asking myself – did I do something to deserve this trauma?

Why is that? Why do we assume that every bad thing that's ever happened to us is our fault? (Or is that just me?) I honestly don't have a great answer for that. I don't have a wise answer to why this shame pitfall is real, I just know it is.

And I can sit in this shame for way too long. And when I sit in this shame, Satan messes with me. He lies. He demeans and degrades me. He deceives me. He accuses me and accuses God. And I can fall into the trap of doing the same.

But there's something powerful about talking about it. Christine has helped me realize that one of my biggest fears is being seen as, or acting like, a "crazy girl." While I'm fine talking about my anxiety, I don't want to be the "drama queen" or a girl who makes "foolish" decisions or who my friends look at like "girl, what are you doing?" That's partly pride. And it's partly my in-securities and fears.

So, when something traumatic happens, my mind goes there first. Does this trauma look "crazy"? Does talking about it make me "dramatic"? Am I a "fool" because I suffered this trauma?

So far, the answer has been "no" in every trauma. Even when my accusers have told me otherwise.

And because the answer is "no," I don't have to be ashamed to talk about it with trusted sisters. I got to talk about this latest one with a wise older sister last night. And we both got to praise God for the victory He's already weaving in that I am already back on my feet and fighting back hell's lies. The situation isn't remedied. I still have a bit of whiplash. It's still something I care about. And I might have residual trauma to deal with. But I'm ok.

This isn't my norm for trauma. Usually this kind of gut-punch would leave me doubled-over for weeks, if not months. I'd be back to crying every day and letting my anger and fear come out side-ways all around me so I'm not here to say that enough prayer and counseling avoids that response to traumatic events. But I will give praise where it's due as I realize my reactions this time can't be explained but for the grace and power of God.

After we shared praises, this sweet friend asked me a question, "do you think we have to be ready to talk about our trauma to be healed?"

I wasn't sure how to answer that question in the moment. And honestly, I'm still not sure there's a "right" answer. But here's what I've come up with.

We don't have to share our trauma to be healed. But if God has healed us, don't we want to share the good news and hope of His healing with others? Again, **NOT** in a willy-nilly fashion. Believe it or not, there are chapters of my story I've chosen not to share in this book. Not because I can't talk about them, but because a book isn't the appropriate platform to do so. A conversation is. I think it's a personal call which traumas fit which bills. Obviously, some of mine found their way into these pages. And some didn't. Those others have been shared in more intimate settings, and I've been a witness to God bringing healing and freedom and security to others in ways I didn't realize hard parts of my story could do.

So, I think the secondary reason that talking about our trauma is important is because Jesus came for the sick, not the healed. We reflect the Gospel when we stand up and say, "me too." When we hear someone say "no, you're not alone, that happened to me too." When a woman we trust and admire says "no, you're not crazy, this is what I'm going through." When a woman we see as a saint says, "here's my story."

No, I don't think we have to share our traumas to be healed. But I think, with wisdom, there can be a lot of freedom and grace given to sisters when we do. I think chains of hell can be broken when a brave woman is willing to share her story with someone who needs to hear it. I think victories happen when we see we don't have to live under the weight of shame for what's happened to us or been done to us.

There's not a one-size-fits-all prescription for when and how and with whom to share. It will take prayer. And wisdom. And a good dose of the Holy Spirit to whisper when maybe you do need to open up as one whose been healed.

Here's my prayer for this chapter – it's threefold. First, I pray this chapter helps you acknowledge trauma faster, in real-time, so you can address it and not get sucked too far into the shame-cycle Satan loves to trap us in. Second, I pray there are women around you who are courageous enough, when the time is appropriate, to share their stories with you so that the grace of God is poured out in your life, and you see He's big enough to handle and heal even "that" – whatever your "that" is. And lastly, I pray if you've been healed, that God would give you a woman, just one sister, to share your story with. To encourage her along this messy journey of life – and that God would bless your obedience in ways you can't imagine as you do so.

We're all going to get knocked down sometimes. And sometimes the blows life delivers will keep us down for a while. But there is victory in seeing our sisters get back up. Sometimes we need to lean on their faith to help us stand again, and sometimes, we need to be the woman with an arm extended, sharing her story of how God put her back on her feet.

Chapter 13

Comparison, the Thief of Joy

As I've been penning these pages, I am living a life that many in this world would classify as "goals." I am a 32-year-old female with an advanced degree, a successful career, a cute apartment, financial security, wonderful family and friends, a great church, my health, and an active lifestyle in the mountains. I have the ability to travel. I have the health to hike, ski and white-water raft in Colorado. And I am surrounded by a truly amazing group of God's people.

On my best days, I look at this list and thank God for His many blessings. But far too often, I look at that list and see what lacks.

And I can create the second list in seconds. No boyfriend, let alone husband. No kids. I'm 32 and still live in an apartment. I think I'm relatively attractive, but I have belly fat, and lovely cellulite that no amount of workouts seem to burn off.

You have a list, too, I'm sure. The things that you don't yet have – but want. Or things you think you're supposed to have "by now" and don't. We all do. Some of the lack is from longings that are good and right and God-given and the waiting seems to kill us. Some of the lack is from circumstances beyond our control which delayed, or even denied our ability to have things we deeply desire.

I have come to see that sometimes lack reveals the perfection we were designed for. We aren't in Eden and the broken world we've inherited is not the perfect masterpiece God originally designed. Since we're not in Eden, we experience lack. We live in a world with less-thans. And sometimes God allows this lack to point us back to Him and remind us that what He offers is better.

But even when the lack reveals good desires, I quickly jump into comparisons. Spend less than a minute scrolling through a social media app and you are bound to find a thousand other things that you don't have to add to your list. A new house, new car, exotic vacation, or perfectly choreographed picture of girlfriends at brunch where everyone looks perfect and has the cutest outfits and not an inch of body fat to be found.

Those posts can frequently trigger my comparison-monster, but it's the dating/wedding/engagement posts that can really make me spiral.

I leap into thoughts of pity. Why don't I have someone who loves me? Why don't I have a doting husband who writes me love notes and brings home flowers just because? Why don't I have a partner who I can't wait to see become a dad? Or who I fall more in love with watching him interact with our children? Where is the man who wants to show me off and posts something sweet about how much he adores me with all of the relevant hashtags to make it all the more clear? The women in these posts must be God's highly favored ones. They have what I long for.

Often, as I keep scrolling, the pity becomes anger. I turn all of these questions to God with a finger pushing into His chest. The woe-is-me tone turns to an indictment. If I lack, God, then surely You aren't good. You don't care about me. You don't love me. Because if You did, I would have this.

And every so often, the scrolling unveils ugly judgment and comparison. It happened to me this week. I saw an engagement post on Instagram, and my thought-train went something like this: 'WHAT – *SHE* IS ENGAGED?! SOMEONE AGREED TO MARRY *HER*?! SHE ISN'T EVEN THAT PRETTY AND IS SO DULL YET I SIT SINGLE?!'

That's not a Godly sentiment, for those keeping score at home – it's ugly. And I am not proud of just how ugly my heart can be. But I promised to be honest. And my heart can get ugly when I sit with the reality of singleness long past when I thought was appropriate. It's not Godly, it's not good, and I'm not justifying it.

But am I the only one whose had that kind of thought? I'm guessing not. I think that reaction is an indicator of the pain we feel in our own lack. And Satan preys on that feeling by bombarding us with opportunities to compare ourselves to the seemingly numerous people who have all that we don't.

My mom always told me that "comparison is the thief of joy." The internet informs me that these wise words were originally attributed to Teddy Roosevelt. No matter who uttered them first, there is wisdom that spans the duration of human existence in that phrase.

While we are perhaps more bombarded with the opportunity for comparison in today's hyper-connected, social media culture, the opportunity was never absent from humanity. We were always a covetous people. It's part of our sinful nature. And probably why God had to put "do not covet" into the 10 Commandments as a top 10 no-no.

Why? Why did God tell us not to be envious and covetous? To not compare ourselves to our neighbor? Probably because it makes us all miserable.

It steals our joy.

It steals our time.

It steals our excitement for others.

It makes us bitter.

I'm not saying that if you just focus on the good stuff in life, all the bad miraculously disappears. While I believe there are many blessings to be found in practicing thankfulness and gratitude to our Creator, you'll never hear me ask someone in the middle of their mess, "what are you thankful for?" Cringe.

Maybe because on this side of heaven, we will not see all of the goodness of the Lord in its fullness. I'm not saying we won't see it. We see some of it. But the Bible says, we see it in part now, but in heaven we'll see it in full (see 1 Corinthians 13). And yet God has given us a lot to enjoy here. A lot to appreciate. A lot to be thankful for. A lot to discover.

We get to make a choice how to live. We can wallow in what isn't right, or we can actively praise the same God who created every single creature on earth. (If you're ever in a bad mood, watch a nature documentary about ocean life – it's hard to be mad at a God who is that wildly creative.)

The reality is we live in a world with less-thans. But comparing my less-than to yours only leads to misery for me. And makes me a lot less kind to you.

So just for today, I am going to focus on the first list – the list of things God has been beyond gracious in providing. And I'm going to keep praying about the second list. The stuff I still long for and lack. And I have a feeling I'm going to be doing that for the rest of my life. But maybe as I keep journeying, I'll trust Him a bit more with the second list, knowing that He provides well. In His time, not mine.

Chapter 14

Singleness in Your 30s

I had moments of panic throughout my 20s, wondering if I was destined to be alone forever, but I could always assuage my fears with the reassurance that I was overreacting. I was still in my 20s after all. I am notoriously impatient, so I would remind myself that my wonderful future husband was out there, God was just spending extra time preparing him for me.

While I complained to God plenty in my 20s, there really was always an underlying optimism (which sometimes got buried under disappointment) that a wonderful man was out there for me.

Singleness at 30 felt different. It felt like I had missed the boat. That all the good ones were taken. Now I was going to have to sort through the 'reject' pile. (Wait – was I now part of that same pile?!) For some reason, in my mind 30 meant that the beautiful love story I dreamed of and prayed for was just going to be messy and hard and less-than now.

To provide perhaps a bit of context for this depressive mood, I turned 30 in Covid-era 2020.

Before I wallow in too much pity, I was super blessed to have been born in September, a time in 2020 when, even in Denver, life had slightly opened up – restaurants were open at limited capacity and people (or at least my people) were being social. I was even more blessed because I had a group of friends and family near and far who were not afraid to get on a plane to celebrate me. My sister and mom came out for a weekend. My best friend for another. I got to ring in my actual 30th (a Wednesday – ew) with sweet girlfriends in a fun restaurant with fancy cocktails.

But the days before and after my birthday were gripped with fear, not of COVID, but of singleness in my 30s.

I had already tried online dating in Denver in bits and spurts in 2019 and was met with deep disappointment. Then I met Chase, who went from the love of my life to a complete sociopath in short order, which really, really messed up my hope. Weeks after our breakup, the world locked down for COVID. And I was six months away from turning 30.

While I wanted to write off men for a while after Chase, for better or worse, 2020 made me want a spouse more, not less. Being alone while the world went mad made me even more desiring of what I now refer to as a "bunker-buddy." Someone to see the world as I do, to be in the bunker of the madness with me, to keep me safe, to share sanity, and fight the lies of this world with me.

I tried dating in 2020 but it was a bust. Let's be real – no one was "thriving" in 2020 (and many weren't even leaving the house) so it was fairly unsurprising that I did not find a man enthusiastic about Jesus, life and me. Now that it's not 2020, I can see that clearly, but in 2020 it felt heavier.

My birthday came and went, and I was still breathing even though singleness loomed large. I'm not sure what it is about the number 30, but it felt like a death sentence. Like I had missed the boat. Like there was nothing left for me. And that feeling came crashing down on me on Christmas.

I was introduced to my sister's new boyfriend at Christmas. I really was super happy for her and was glad she had met a man she was excited about. But somewhere in the back of my head, fear gripped me with this startling thought – "I am going to be alone forever, this is my new reality. I'm now a fifth-wheel in my own family." And the floodgates of tears opened.

I had to awkwardly excuse myself from Christmas caroling around the piano to run upstairs and lock myself in a bathroom and cry rivers of tears over the prospective grief that thought brought. A fitting way to end 2020.

In the days after Christmas, as I unraveled my feelings that had led to an overwhelming sense of despair, I realized that for some reason, the number 30 really did feel like a death sentence to the possibility of finding the man I longed for. That's not logical, I know, but it felt different. As I neared 31, those feelings re-emerged.

Right before my 31st birthday, I had this overwhelming sense I was getting old. Because of my hair. Yes, that's kind of vain, but hear me out.

The one thing throughout my life that I always felt was beautiful about me was my hair. A sweet hairdresser once told me it was my "crown of glory." (And yes, I've hung on to that compliment that was probably given when I was in high school!) But throwing modesty out the window, I'll just say it – I was blessed with good hair. My belly fat came and went, and I was periodically insecure about the cellulite on my bottom half, but my hair was always my crown – and a bigger source of my sense of beauty than I realized.

The stress of law school (and genetics) gave me my first few grey hairs in my mid-20s. While I didn't love it then, the greys were few – like count on one hand few – so I didn't care too much. I had gotten a few more over the rest of my 20s, but they came in strong in 2020. (Thank you 2020, for another lovely gut punch.)

I had never dyed my hair (again, it was good hair) and while I was really starting to hate the amount of grey I saw, I really didn't want to dye it. Somewhere along the line, I stubbornly decided "well, I'm actually getting older, maybe I should just accept it." As my sister can tell you, it was a stubborn, grouchy "acceptance."

What was hidden underneath my faux acceptance was grief, anger, and fear. I was afraid of getting older – not because I fear getting older itself, but because I feared doing it alone. My hair greying to the point of noticeability made me realize I was getting older and was a daily reminder that I was still single. Which led to anger. Anger that my husband had not yet arrived. Anger that I was great, but still waiting. Anger that some of my youth would be lost by the time I got married and had kids.

While I never planned on being married early, my plan had involved marriage in my late 20s. But that plan didn't happen. What I'm now living wasn't how I pictured my life playing out. And that's led to grief. Some of my dreams for my life have died – or at least my vision for when and how they should happen have died. Grief by its definition is a response to loss. I lost how I thought my journey to my future husband was 'supposed' to go.

I read once that we don't have funerals for dead dreams. But maybe we should. Or at least should have the space to grieve them. For many of us, our singleness unearths dead or dying dreams. The pictures we had as little girls of what life would look like in our 20s and 30s was a starkly different picture than what we face in the reality of those years. We have to let go of how we "thought" life would be here, and face what it is. That's a process for many of us. And it's a choice. I can complain daily to God that I'm single at 32. (And there are days that happens.) Or I can ask, God, what do you have for me today? The latter is risky.

What if today holds more singleness? What if He leads me in a direction I wasn't planning on? What if He doesn't provide what I think I need?

While I still have plenty of days where I don't *feel* this, what I **KNOW** is that God will give me everything I need, for today. The Bible says so. And God cannot lie.

He will give me enough for today. And sometimes, not a drop more. Other days, He'll fill my cup so full that I'm brimming over for weeks. But He sees every day. He cares about every day. He knows how much I long for a husband, a partner on this journey. And I truly believe He cares.

On my best days, I believe that He's preparing me for that journey, and a special man for me. But when the singleness continues, and feels too long and too hard, I can despair. I can't say I have a lot of wisdom beyond that. That's the real fluctuation of my heart as I sit in the singleness past when I thought it should end. But I know God has plans for this season. (I mean, if you're reading this, these words were part of the plan for this season.)

So just for today, I'm going to lean in and trust He writes better stories than I do. He's creative, He's good, and He's for me. So my continued singleness is part of the story. And He'll use it for my good. (That said, if you happen to know my future husband and want to give him a nudge to get moving, I won't complain.)

Chapter 15

The Weight of Disappointment

*I*t's hitting again. That wave of grief, followed by anger, that I've come to find is an indication of my disappointment.

This time it's because of a job. An employer that I once thought I'd retire with, but who is not who I wanted them to be. So, I began writing this chapter on the morning of my last day with this employer, after a night without sleep, my emotional exhaustion peaking.

I've left jobs before. But the others were places I wanted to get out of as soon as I stepped in the door. This is one that I really thought would last forever. One where I'm leaving some really wonderful people behind.

That's different. And hard. Honestly, it's disappointing.

I'm no stranger to disappointment – clearly my love life has had plenty. But my job was the area of my life that for the past several years, I got to chalk up as a win.

You know what I mean, right? Sometimes the rest of life is falling to shambles, but God graciously provides one area that feels like a success – that feels stable, that feels safe. This place saw me through some dark, difficult years. During a season where many of the stories in this book were birthed, my workplace was my safe place. And I think that's the grief that's hitting.

To lose those once safe places, or people, or things, that brought comfort – even sanity – during a chaotic season – honestly – it can be devastating, and sometimes harder to process than the season it saw us through.

I guess in that way I'm lucky. I became aware of my disappointment in this workplace several months ago. And God, in His deep grace, convicted me to stay for a while longer, and not flee at the first wave of disappointment. I can see clearly now that a major reason for that was to let me grieve it properly. To let me sit in the disappointment. To let me process what that disappointment meant, and why, exactly, I was disappointed.

Not every season has time for that. Sometimes we're disappointed but we have to move forward. Sometimes we're disappointed and it takes us time (sometimes a long time) to figure out what that emotion is.

But this season gave me that, and I've learned some things sitting in it.

For starters, I really hate disappointment. Disappointment makes me angry. It makes me sad. And I just really don't want to be disappointed.

Why is that? Why does disappointment cause me so much pain? Likely in part because I am loyal to a fault, and I want people and places to come through for me. I want people and places to be trustworthy. I want things I can believe in. And every time I face disappointment, I'm forced to remember this world – the people and things in it – will all disappoint. I know that. I'm 32 – I've seen it. But every time I see it, I get hit hard. I'm not totally sure why. (Christine hasn't graced me with that insight yet.) Disappointment hits me hard and I hate it.

Relatedly, I've realized I often don't know what to do with disappointment. Part of me wants to lash out against those who disappoint me. Part of me wants to never see them again. Part of me wants to dive back in and try to correct the problem because surely they didn't mean to disappoint me, and if they only knew the source of my disappointment, they'd correct it.

The last option is the cycle I found myself in with this job. I was blessed to have a good relationship with my bosses, and open dialogue about the direction of the company. Unfortunately, over time, I found that while these people enjoyed my praise, they were deaf to any constructive criticism. Thankfully, wisdom finally reminded me that insanity is repeating the same thing and expecting a different result – that if I couldn't live with how things were, seeing that those in power were not going to change anything, I needed to leave.

Honestly, this made me angry. And I found out (or was reintroduced to the fact) that I am not a fun person when I'm disappointed. As previously mentioned, I'm angry when I'm disappointed. And unfortunately, that anger often comes out sideways on the people around me who had nothing to do with the source of the disappointment.

Why is it so hard to just address the person or place that disappointed us rather than let that disappointment broil within us until it boils over onto everyone else who doesn't deserve it? For me, I think it's because I overanalyze most things, so it takes me a while to actually realize someone disappointed me. I often place the blame on myself first before accepting that someone else let me down. I have major Enneagram "2" energy so the idea of people not caring as much as I do is disappointing, and I think my misguided coping mechanism is to put the responsibility for disappointment solely on my shoulders so I don't have to deal with someone else actually disappointing me. I don't recommend it. It's not a great coping mechanism. 0/5 stars.

People will disappoint us. Even people closest to us. Because they're human. And part of living in a broken world is learning how to mend things that are broken.

And part of living in a broken world is learning how to deal with the disappointment and being able to move forward in hope.

"Everything here will disappoint. Everything here, even the best things, will fall short. Lord, instead of letting that fill me with anger or despair, let me see You. Let me see Your kindness in being an anchor for my soul. Let me hope for the promises You gave – to renew all things, to restore what the locusts have eaten, to never leave or forsake me. In Your ways. Which are so much more beautiful than my ways. You've always provided. You will here, too."

I think, just maybe, disappointment is an invitation from the Father. (And trust me, I hated typing that as much as you might have cringed reading it.) Disappointment forces me to address the fact that this world is not home. It is disappointing. It is broken. It is messy. And often it's dark.

Rather than trying to fix it all on my own, rather than trying to trick my brain into really thinking "it's okay – it doesn't bother me – I'm just being unreasonable," maybe God is asking me to bring it to Him. To say "hey God, this happened and I'm disappointed. This person treated me this way, and it's not okay. This world is broken, and it's not okay. This dream died, and I'm disappointed."

Maybe He sees my grief ... and maybe ... maybe He grieves with me. I mean, He's perfect. He doesn't revel in His creation going astray, He surely doesn't delight in His perfect world being tarnished by evil. Maybe the ability to be disappointed is proof I'm an eternal being – that something deep in my soul knows this isn't how things should be. That I was designed for much better.

That won't take away the disappointment. It doesn't mean that life's crushing blows don't sometimes cripple me, don't knock the wind out of me. They do and they will. But I'm learning to see God in the highs and the lows. He's with me in the depths of despair. He's with me in disappointment. Even when it's heavy and it hurts. He's with you there, too. He might not feel there (I know those seasons well), but He is. Ask God to sit with you there. In the weight of disappointment. He will.

Chapter 16

2020

*I*f you weren't single during the-year-the-world-went-mad, you had your own struggles. I know that parenting and marriage weren't walks in the park during this season. But being single – especially if you lived alone – was a uniquely hellish experience in 2020.

The world has always had evil, but 2020 made the evil feel realer, closer – imminent to me.

For the first time in my life, I had a daily sense that I was not safe. That the world was not safe. For me, it had nothing to do with the coronavirus itself, but everything to do with how the world reacted to it. I lived in downtown Denver at the start of the pandemic and watched a thriving city turn into a ghost town. The roads cleared, the sidewalks were deserted and nearly every restaurant or business I had regularly frequented were not just shut down, they were boarded up. My brain couldn't make sense of it. I had just been in this bar a few weeks ago – now it looked like it had been abandoned or had survived an apocalypse. Where were the baristas that I knew by name at this coffee shop whose two-story glass windows were now covered with plywood and "DO NOT ENTER" signs?

Downtown Denver looked post-apocalyptic for much of the summer of 2020. I lived a few blocks away from the capital building, which BLM protesters took over for much of the summer. On a few occasions I saw massive swarms of police in riot gear hanging onto tanks riding into downtown Denver. It felt like a war scene.

People who lived in the suburbs never had to see this. They worked from home until they were told to come back (usually not until 2021 or later) and never saw this crazy change, nor felt the sting of it daily. But I did. Because single people lived downtown. And they lived alone. So we got to experience this hellish year in a unique way.

I think it was a time of profound loneliness for everyone, but I happened to be painfully aware of it from the start, in part because I had just had a traumatic ending with Chase a few weeks earlier. I was already reeling from the pain of a relationship failing, being alone again, and being extremely confused and angry about why God had allowed it. I needed people around me. I needed to not be alone.

But instead, we had lock-downs. If you were single, COVID brought **_legally mandated loneliness_**. You weren't supposed to go anywhere or do anything. You weren't allowed to see anyone outside your "household." My household was me, myself, and I. Cue music for "lonely, I am so lonely."

I was lucky. I had a few friends who agreed to 'illegally' see each other even in the early days of the pandemic. I was a rule-abiding citizen until COVID. But loneliness literally drove me to break the law (or guidelines or mandates or whatever they were). And in my world, it was mostly single people who I saw banding together like this. Frankly, it was single people who needed to. Married people had each other. And often had family or couple friends that they "huddled up" with. But single people, living alone, far from family across multiple state lines didn't have that option.

Look, COVID or not, it's not healthy to be by yourself in an apartment for 24 hours a day 7 days a week. No one to talk to. No one to see. No one to hug. It's enough to make anyone lose their mind. And those of us who realized the risk of serious depression might be much more dangerous than the risk of COVID, well, we banded together. And shared a common language. Of feeling like social lepers for "bucking" the system. For feeling shamed for wanting, no needing, social interaction. And a dang hug.

I know that the six feet of distance and masks and all the other anti-social behavior that came with COVID was hard on everyone. But I'm going to humbly submit that it was a unique damnation for singles. Because where were we supposed to go? We weren't just alone, we were shunned. This wasn't a loneliness you could escape from. You literally weren't welcome. Anywhere.

"I'm sick of being isolated. It's frustrating that those with spouses and significant others are so easily staying home and avoiding others when some of us are alone and lonely. I am alone and lonely. And I am sick of feeling like a rebel and a leper for wanting human interaction. It's hard not to take people's hysteria personally."

You craved human interaction, you longed for people. But you sat alone. And couldn't ask for help. Because you weren't supposed to see people. It was our national duty to be alone. It was patriotism. It was 'caring for your neighbor'. If you rebelled, you were told you might kill someone! That is psychologically damaging.

As I write this chapter, I still see the impacts that this year of loneliness caused. I still see a world around me that is traumatized by the "renormalization" of 2020. I still see us "othering" each other for healthcare choices. I still see shame being used as a mighty weapon of conformity. And it's ugly.

Let me be clear, with some time and perspective, I can recognize that not everything about 2020 was bad. I think Americans collectively have a changed relationship with work, and that's honestly a really good thing. People spent time with their families instead of being at work 24/7 and I hope and pray some families were healed because of that.

But for a lot of us, the bad in 2020 far outweighed the good in our personal lives, and I don't think it's stuff we can gloss over. Because for some of us, it wasn't stuff our hearts could so easily bounce back from.

We relearned how to socialize, how to interact, and questioned if we even should. We saw other humans as the "enemy," as literal "threats" to our lives. That's crazy. No way does that make for good mental health. It's no surprise that suicide rates have sky-rocketed since.

The damage Satan did through this still makes me mad to my core. It makes me furious. Because there were (and maybe are) a lot of single people who felt like garbage because of how we justified treating them during COVID. And I'll humbly submit that many of us felt alone, we felt unwanted, we felt uncared for, we felt like outcasts. It was overwhelming.

I didn't know how much anger I had in me until 2020. But I was **_ANGRY_**.

I was angry the world was mad. I was angry liberties that my profession exists to uphold were summarily stripped away. I was angry there was so much fear. I was angry there was so much division. I was angry that I was alone. I was angry that I felt shamed for needing people – physically present people. I was angry that church doors were closed in a season I felt I needed community most. I was angry I was single. I was angry about a lot.

I'm not good at stuffing emotions. And honestly, I usually don't. But somewhere along the lines I had seen anger as a "bad" emotion, one good Christians didn't have. One that seemed harder to talk about. And so, while I didn't consciously stuff it, I just tried not to acknowledge it. (That's probably semantics but let me have it.)

I think part of the reason anger seemed "bad" to me was because I hadn't seen anger modeled well. Usually when people get angry, it comes out sideways all over the people around them, and it's ugly. I didn't want to be that person.

But in 2020, I had a lot of time to consciously sit in my anger. And because I can't ignore a problem I'm aware of (thank you over-active brain), I had to address it. So, I turned to where I usually turn first – books. (I'm a first child and a big fan of learning from other people's mistakes or wisdom before I mess up big on my own.) I'm sure there are a million great books out there on biblical anger, but my Amazon search was very literal and Gary Chapman's "Anger: Taming a Powerful Emotion" popped up first in my search. Thanks to Prime delivery, I had guidance in my hands two days later. I won't regurgitate Gary's book (but highly recommend it if this chapter is hitting a nerve), but want to highlight the larger take-away that I think we should address: anger isn't a right or wrong, good or bad emotion, it's an indicator emotion — it points to something that we perceive as being wrong — unjust, unfair, unloving. It's actually a God-designed emotion that as we possess as soul-having creatures.

Anger is actually a gift.

It's meant to tell us something is off. Either in our circumstances or within us.

2020 was off. Majorly off. And my emotions told me that early on.

As I type these words, the world is still off. While nothing in my world has been locked down for over a year, the trauma from 2020 still reverberates within and around me. COVID has not ceased to exist. Neither politicians nor vaccines were able to "stop" it. There's still fear, still anger, still shaming, still division. And I still hate it. And still get angry about it.

That's all. I don't have a solution for it. I know Satan has used this to isolate us, to divide us. And I pray God is doing more than I see in the spiritual realms because the earthly ones have looked pretty bleak these past few years. But after a year+ of sitting in the dark season caused by 2020 and a pandemic, I felt I would be remiss if I didn't share my impressions of this season with you. Because I don't think I am the only person who experienced 2020 single. I don't think I'm the only person who felt angry. I don't think I'm the only person who felt that everything was off. So, if you had those feelings, too, you weren't alone. You weren't crazy.

Sometimes, we don't need people to fix the world for us, we just need to know we're not alone in it.

Chapter 17

Hell Hates You

I think it's important we talk about the hidden antagonist that lurks around the fringes of every chapter of the story.

I have an enemy. A real enemy. It isn't my singleness, it isn't COVID, it isn't a bad employer, it isn't Instagram, and it isn't toxic men.

According to the Bible, my enemy is the schemes, the rulers and the principalities of hell. It's Satan. As with any good enemy, Satan hates me. And he hates you too.

While there are far wiser authors who have dedicated whole books to the subject of Satan and the schemes of hell, I think it's important to touch on this reality in a book about hope in the desert. I am convinced that sometimes we get stuck in the valleys longer than we need to because we don't realize we have an adversary.

So let me be clear, you have an enemy – a real one.

His name is Satan, or the Devil. 1 Peter 5:8 says that "[our] enemy the devil prowls around like a roaring lion looking for someone to devour." I don't know how many nature documentaries you've watched, but if you have ever seen a lion stalking its prey, even if the prey manages to run away once, the lion usually manages to take a weaker animal out. Since I believe the Bible is the inspired word of God, I think God had a point to make by comparing Satan to a roaring lion looking for prey.

Satan is out for destruction. He's hungry for it. His aim is to destroy anything that God said is good. Which means if Satan has his way, you are not going to experience life to the full. If Satan has his druthers, you won't have hope, you won't heal, and you'll never get out of the desert.

See Satan and God had a big fight a long time ago and Satan lost – big time. Satan used to be an angel, but then decided he should actually be God. God did not agree. Satan was kicked out of heaven and God had a lot to say about Satan's impending doom. For reasons I can't explain, God didn't destroy Satan then. He spared Satan for now. Which means Satan is allowed to continue roaming the earth stalking God's people.

Time-Out:

I totally acknowledge that leaves room for a thousand questions about what God allows. I can go down that rabbit hole as fast as anyone. If God allowed Satan to continue roaming the earth, then has God purposely allowed the pain and destruction Satan causes? Were those things then the will of God? Does God cause evil? Did he cause the evil that's been allowed in my life?!

I'm not a theologian, a pastor or any manner of professional on the Bible – just a girl following Jesus – but here's what I've come up with so far.

God doesn't cause evil.

He can't. It's not in His nature. But He does allow it.

He is 100% over everything that happens in heaven and on earth and He can control all of it. But for reasons I can't comprehend in this flesh-suit I'm in, He doesn't always intervene when evil rears its ugly head. Personally, I think in part, it's because we rebelled and chose to live outside of the perfection of Eden.

I also think God still allows evil because He is really good at re-demption. And in order to redeem, there has to be something broken to redeem.

I realize this doesn't explain away horror. It might not even help. It's just my humble submission of how I've reconciled a God who could make everything perfect right now, who chooses not to. You are free to take it or leave it. God is big enough for your questions. He's got answers that I don't. So, keep asking. Even if you need to yell to ask. Back to our regularly-scheduled programming.

In this epic heavenly conflict, I think it's important to recognize Satan lost then, and has been promised ultimate defeat. Which means the war is won.

God defeated Satan on the Cross. We are no longer separated from God. Jesus made a way. Hell doesn't get the final say. That is something to celebrate! We have freedom from the bondage of hell – thank you Jesus!

But there are still battles to be fought between here and eternity.

Satan is a sore loser. He knows he can't defeat God, that ship has sailed. So instead, Satan goes after us – God's image bearers. Basically, Satan knows the war is over, but he wants to inflict as much harm as he can until God says "no more." Yes, that's sadistic – that is Satan's whole thing.

While I don't know when the day is when God says "no more" and deals the final deathblow to Satan, I do know that God gave us the power, through Jesus Christ and His Holy Spirit living in us, to defeat Satan in the earthly battles that face us.

So let's talk about the battles.

Satan's attacks are deceptive – he's called the father of lies. His plan is to manipulate Truth – about God and about your identity. While Satan is tricky, he's not original. He has patterns.

One pattern of hell is distraction. Satan loves to distract us. He distracted Eve from the abundance of Eden, and he distracts us, too. He sends what the Bible calls flaming arrows into our lives (a nasty email from a boss, a fender bender, a broken water heater). Often, these arrows are not actually meant to kill us or destroy us, they're meant to distract us. I don't know about you, but I can start the day ready to take on the world, and quickly lose steam when one relatively small thing goes wrong. All the more when crisis or chaos hits. I quickly forget how good my God is when I feel the pricks and pulls of the darkness of this world.

Satan knows that.

He isn't all-knowing, like God, but he knows our patterns. He can plot out our weaknesses and fears. And he preys on them. Satan fully intends to take advantage of them. Because he knows he can't destroy you. So he intends to make you miserable instead.

Satan's goal is to make your time on earth futile and unproductive. Satan wants to suffocate you with sin, insecurity, fear and despair until you are completely crippled. Satan's ultimate desire is to separate you from God. He doesn't care if it's through apathy or through active separation. He just wants you to be separate from God.

It's all part of his larger agenda – he wants to get you to a place where you're not actively listening to and obeying the voice of God, let alone walking in faith.

Faith makes hell tremble.

So the powers of hell will make you too busy to spend time with God. Or Satan will convince you that the questions you have about God defeat any purpose in continuing to seek Him. Satan will try to make you think that it's unproductive to be a woman of faith in the 21st century, with so much logic and science around. He will zero in on your deepest desires and insecurities and will promise to show you a way to achieve them or heal them while bypassing God. He's got different strategies for different people, but they all end up in the same place – separating you from God.

While Satan often uses distractions and detours, Satan loves to steal, too.

Of all the things he loves to steal, peace is at the top of the list. He wants us to be anxious, worried, fearful and constantly in turmoil. We're not big threats if we're crippled by a lack of peace.

But the Gospel calls us to peace, not fear. In fact, fear is another strategy of hell. God says "do not fear." Satan says "fear." Whenever fear is present in your life, you can be certain that the enemy is nearby.

As I mentioned in talking about sexuality and my experience with Alan and my bout with deep depression, Satan knows my trigger points. And he uses them against me. I've realized over the years that often, he sends hoards of arrows when God is about to do something in me or through me that will benefit His Kingdom. Hell hates God's Kingdom and is still trying to destroy it. And whenever I'm walking in faith and obedience, I should expect spiritual warfare.

But we can fight back. We're going to have battles on this earth, but we know who wins the war. Which means we fight from a place of victory.

Shalom is the Hebrew word for peace. Interestingly, shalom does not refer to the absence of chaos. Instead, it refers to a deeply entrenched sense of harmony and wholeness, in the ***midst*** of chaos.

I'll be honest, you have to fight for peace. It doesn't just show up one day and stick around forever. While peace is a gift of God, we have to defend it. We have to actively seek it.

We're given spiritual armor to put on daily to walk into battle. The belt of Truth. The breastplate of righteousness. The sandals of peace. The helmet of salvation. The sword of the Spirit. And prayer. I'm not going to walk through these pieces of armor, but highly recommend studying them (there are great books written on this subject).

Because we have armor, we don't just fight defensively. While arguably, the best offense is a good defense, when we get in a defensive groove, we'll find that we can actually move forward – we can take back enemy-occupied territory. As Jesus-followers, we're called to play offense. We are invited to bring pieces of heaven down to earth. In God's strength, and with our armor secured, we can actually start taking back territory Satan sought to steal from us and the people and places we love.

Whether you claim it or not, your identity is warrior princess. You are a child of God and you have been given His authority to fight the schemes of hell.

But you must first recognize the battle. The crap happening in your life isn't accidental. It's got Satan's fingerprints all over it. See, nothing here is the real enemy.

Our real battle is not what we can see with our eyes. It's not against "flesh and blood" (aka earthly things or people) but against the "rulers, the authorities, and the powers of the dark world" and the "spiritual forces of evil in the heavenly realms."

Hell hates you! It's scheming against you. And I hope that makes you a little (or a lot) mad. To know you've been getting kicked around by a punk named Satan. To realize the lies of worthlessness have been a strategic ploy to keep you crippled and useless. To see that the people in your life who drive you nuts aren't the real enemy – Satan is purposely creating division in your relationships to distract you.

I pray you take this to heart and start fighting back.

Hell doesn't expect us to recognize its schemes. Let alone expect us to fight back. But we can. And we have the power of the One who has already won on our side.

Being aware of the schemes of hell will not prevent Satan's attacks nor will it insulate your life from tragedy. But seeing how Satan uses devastation in and around you does produce freedom. It does allow you to commune with God more intimately.

And it will produce fruit, including shalom – peace, even amid the chaos.

Part III

STILL IN THE DESERT…
AND A FEW LESSONS
ALONG THE WAY

Chapter 18

Wrestling with God

As I've mentioned, I was blessed to have found my counselor, Christine, a few weeks before Sean and I broke up. Christine had only a few sessions to get caught up with my life (and what I *thought* were my biggest issues) before my ending with Sean unleashed years of tears and grief I hadn't yet processed.

Christine gave me space to process. I have a very verbal family and we have lots of opinions of the 'right' ways to do most things. Including feel. And grieve. And mourn. And change. I often felt suffocated by the expectations of how I thought I was supposed to handle all of the feelings that were pent up behind years of being too busy (and too focused) to address them.

As I've realized over the years, Christine gave me two gifts in that season – uncaring and unknowing. Those don't sound like gifts, and certainly don't sound like something a Christian could (or should) give to another believer, but they were – and still are.

Christine cares about me – she even prays for me – but she's not a regular, participating member of my daily life. She isn't personally impacted by my decisions, good or bad. And that allows her the freedom, at some level, to "not care" about the direction I choose or the day-to-day choices I make. Since they do not impact her on a relational level, she can "uncare" about them. She is for me and is invested in my healing but doesn't have a vision for my life. She gets to hold space for me to process my journey, without being personally affected by how my process unfolds.

Christine also taught me the precious gift of "unknowing." Unknowing is the space where someone is for you, and wants Jesus to be the center of your life, but recognizes that they don't know what Jesus is actually, actively doing in your life. Instead of telling me what Jesus is saying to me, she asks questions to help me unlock those answers. (And sometimes challenges me and speaks prophetic wisdom over me.)

There's a serious faith in that. Faith that God has a plan for me. Faith that He can tell me what it is. And faith that she doesn't need to actively intervene, just facilitate. She isn't my Holy Spirit, but she encourages me to seek Him out. (I pray you find yourself a counselor that not only points you to Jesus and gently walks with you through the pain, find a woman who speaks Truth to you, even when you don't want to hear it, and challenges you to deeper faith.)

Because of the sweet gifts of "uncaring" and "unknowing," somewhere along the lines, Christine gave me a freedom I hadn't heard within church walls up to that point. I was allowed to question God's plan.

I was allowed to wrestle with God.

She pointed me to the biblical model of Jacob, who literally wrestled with God and had his hip socket dislocated. She also pointed me to Jesus himself, who, in the Garden of Gethsemane, before the Cross, asked if the cup (aka death – by crucifixion – on a cross) could be taken from Him. Being God, He was able to in that moment say "yet not as I will, but as You will." (Matthew 26:39).

And because that's what Jesus did, that's the model for Christians.

But we don't always get to the "yet not my will, but Yours" immediately. Actually, I would argue, we often speak those words as "correct" theology but don't know them deeply. Haven't waded into the waters of "if not" deep enough to uncover the questions and the pain and the difficulty if God doesn't take the cup from us. If He allows death before resurrection. If He doesn't redeem the situation how we want Him to. If He doesn't remove the difficult season. If He doesn't heal us as soon as we'd like. If He doesn't move the mountain. If He doesn't ... fill in the blank.

Christine wisely gave me the space and freedom to enter into these questions. To attempt to discover who God is if His answer is no. Or if His answer is silence. Or if He allows the unthinkable. I mean, He allowed His only Son to die a horrifying, painful death. And He's good. And He used it for good. But what if He allows that level of pain in my life?

I have spent a lot of my life trying to avoid that kind of pain. And I can see now, while it's partly because I don't have a high pain tolerance, it's mostly because I didn't want to have to wrestle with those questions. I knew my faith didn't go that deep. At least it didn't then.

But God, in His infinite wisdom, has allowed deep pain, heartache, loss and trauma in my young life. Not because He's cruel. But in order to show me new sides of Himself. To show me how big He is.

God is small when life is safe.

So, in His grace, He chose to allow pain to enter my life to show me He truly can move mountains. He can rescue. He can redeem.

We can't know redemption unless we have things that need redeemed.

I'm sitting with that sentence, too. Because it's beautiful. And it's ugly. It's beautiful to know a God who can redeem. But it's anything but lovely to have pieces that still need healing and redemption – it's a painful reminder that all is not well here.

We live in brokenness. We experience decay. We live in the "less thans." And God's offer isn't to take that all away at this very moment. His offer is a promise – that He will.

When?

When will He heal the sick parts of my life? When will He restore what seasons of life have taken? When will He redeem the still broken parts?

I don't know.

Maybe today. Maybe tomorrow. Maybe in 6 months. Maybe in 6 years. Maybe not on this side of eternity.

I struggle with that Truth, too. I'm a control freak – I want to know when and how and where my Heavenly Father is going to come through. I seriously believe He will, but I want to know the details.

Really, I want to brace myself for His goodness being long. It's one thing if He delivers tomorrow. But 6 months is a long way off. 6 years is longer. And what if – what if He doesn't deliver redemption on this side of eternity?

I'll be honest, I jump to the last possibility as soon as the redemption doesn't happen yesterday. (I am aware that my thorn-in-the-flesh is impatience – God and I are working on it. Okay ... He's **graciously** providing opportunities for me to uncomfortably learn it.) But honestly, I jump to the worst case as a means of control, not of trust. If I can wrap my head around a good God not coming through for a long long time (and many more 'longs' if we're waiting until eternity), then I can still 'trust' Him.

While this might sound godly, it's not. At least, not for me. Because the only way I can even begin to wrap my head around it is to go cold. While it is theologically true that even if I never see another blessing, another glimpse of God's redemptive, restorative plan on this side of Heaven, He is still good, and is still good to me – that's not a Truth I can feel. My heart just wasn't made for that. In trying to believe that I go into the head-knowledge of God and shut off my heart. But then I miss the relational God that is the whole point of the Gospel.

Honestly, I don't think God asked me to wrap my head around His timing to be spiritually mature, or a Christian at all. But I try to. And when I can't (every time I try), I spiral. I doubt God's goodness. I question the depth of my faith. I try to be stoic and say I don't care about these deepest longings of my heart – I can live without them because God is enough. And then I get angry that I still have the unmet longings.

As my pastor would say, "can we take a time out here?"

I don't think God has asked me to figure out His timing. Or to be completely okay with it being outside of my comprehension. I don't think He's upset I have earthly longings. He knows I'm frail. He knows I'm weak. All of heaven and earth know I'm impatient.

But I think God smiles at my wrestling. And my questioning.

Actually, I know He does. Why? Because wrestling and questioning invites Him into the realest, deepest, most vulnerable parts of me. To the big questions. To the big pain. And God, being God, will not force me to expose those parts. He knows them without my revealing them, but He won't force me to trust Him. He won't force me to let Him in. God is a gentleman.

As a gentleman, when I start to reveal my deep questions, my messy heart, He sees beauty, not chaos. It's part of who God is. It's why we love the romantic comedies where a "hot mess" wins over the calm, steady, handsome prince. Because our hearts were made for that type of acceptance and love.

My wrestling with God isn't annoying to Him, it's lovely. It isn't putting Him out. He isn't sighing, wishing I'd just understand all of heaven and earth already. He's smiling. Inviting me to a deeper knowledge of Him. Not of His timing, necessarily. Not of the answers to all of my questions. Just to Him. And somewhere in this wrestling match, I find peace.

Not because I know the future. Not because I know how much pain He'll allow. Not because I know how or when He redeems the time spent waiting. Simply because I know Him.

I heard recently that faith is believing that if we knew all that God knew, we'd say "of course" to His timing. I think that's beautiful. To consider that if I was sitting next to God and could comprehend all of human history and everything to come, I'd say "yes" to everything that has happened thus far. It's honestly a wild thought.

And I think the wrestling gets us there. To the point where we can read that and say, yeah, that's right. I don't necessarily feel it in everything yet, but I see a lot of places looking back where God had to allow that redirection, that hurt, that disappointment, even that pain, to get me to where He wanted me, to show me His glory, to unveil His favor and anointing on my life. This book was birthed through pain. Years that I thought would be my ruin, He's instead turning into jewels in my crown.

I don't know what you're wrestling with. I don't know what big questions you have of God or what big pain you've faced. But keep wrestling. Keep asking. We're only really honest with the people we love and trust. So be honest with God. You are moving the heart of God by entering into a sacred space of wrestling with God. Of asking big questions. And even exposing the deep anger and pain. Ask with honesty, ask with vulnerability. Be angry, be sad. Wrestle through it. He's big enough for it. And loves that you're willing to take it to Him.

Chapter 19

Jesus Heals, Time Helps

A few days ago I stood on top of a mountain. That's not really note-worthy in itself since I live in Colorado and frequently get to stand on mountains. But this mountain was special.

I hadn't been to the top of it since my first visit to Colorado, in the summer of 2013, when my dad 'won' and my mom allowed us to go west for a summer vacation, rather than to the beaches of South Carolina or Florida where vacation usually found us. My dad planned an amazing tour of Colorado for our family that summer – hiking, white-water rafting, a train-ride to the top of a mountain, and so much more. I fell in love with Colorado that summer.

And I vividly remember standing on top of this particular mountain during that trip. It was the summer before I started law school. It was before anxiety became my companion, before I ever met any of my future boyfriends, before real heartbreak, before much of this book's stories were lived. But something stands out about what I felt clearly then – Colorado had some place in my story, and perhaps even in my romantic journey.

When I met Daniel and found out his family summered and wintered in Colorado, I thought he was the answer to that feeling I had on top of Pike's Peak. When we broke up, it felt like maybe that part of the journey (and dream) was over, too. It took a few years to go back to Colorado after our breakup. I thought it was a place of pain and trauma. And wasn't sure I could step foot into the Denver Airport without bursting into tears.

Instead, Colorado became home. It has seen some of my biggest victories and my deepest traumas. It has seen heartache and heartbreak. But it has also birthed new fruit. Deeper relationships. Big wins. New wine. A fresher look at the God who saw all of it beforehand and has held me every step of the way.

Sometimes my impatient heart needs time. Though I hate waiting, sometimes only time can provide the perspective needed to see God's goodness throughout the journey. It doesn't make every part of my story in and of itself good. The hurts and traumas were not, in themselves, good. But I see God's protection, and even favor, in spite of them. I have seen God do miracles and redeem some of the heartbreaks and traumas.

Remember that awful job I was dying in when I got to Colorado? God provided a good way out after only 4 months at that job. And that new place became a good home for three years of my professional life. It was a safe place professionally while I was emotionally unraveling. I found out that despite what previous jobs had implied, I was actually a good attorney, and maybe even a good leader. But sometimes good things are for a season, not forever, and I had to let go of what that employer was not, and the ways that place was not beneficial for me long-term. God gave me time to grieve that before I left, because it truly was a loss. Whether it's a job, a relationship, a dream – things not being what we desired them to be creates loss. And the natural reaction to loss is grief. In the middle of grief, it's hard to see clearly. But God can redeem all of it.

Because God likes to show off, my next job was literally one floor above hell, in the same building as my hellish, soul-sucking, nearly-killed-me, made-me-want-to-quit-law job that I had when I first got to Colorado. But one floor higher. It was a God-wink, that God can take anything broken, anything awful, and raise me out of it. In this case, God literally lifted me just a few feet out of my own personal form of hell. And so I remember how much He's done – how much He's healed and redeemed in my professional identity. If He can do that, what else can He do?

While God is able to heal things in an instant, I've seen He often chooses to do so slowly. Methodically. Using time as part of the prescription for healing. Jesus heals. But sometimes we need to allow Him time to heal us. And I think it's often because we aren't actually ready for healing all-at-once. It would be too much. A shock to the system.

So God gives us healing over time. Time allows us to see the healing. Time allows our brains some space to comprehend the healing. Time allows us to appreciate it. Time gives space to see how far He brought us.

Time gives space to see people and situations with new eyes. Years later, I'm beyond grateful I am not married to Daniel. Years later, I can see why Sean and I were not right either, though I still think incredibly highly of him (and am grateful to have received his blessing on his place in this book).

I am utterly convinced that God is on a mission to redeem. More often than not I'd prefer Him to make my life one that avoids things that need redemption, but I'm learning it's a gift He hasn't made my life shatter-proof. He brings great beauty through broken things restored. Redeemed. Made new. He promises to restore what the locusts have eaten (Joel 2:25). He has the power to raise the dead to life. So He has the power to breathe life into the dead parts of our souls as well.

I see Him clearer when He comes through in a situation where hope seems lost. I trust Him more when I see Him deliver things, beautiful things, without my prompting, pushing, or even asking.

Now, let's be clear, I'm no saint. While I have mountaintop days (literally) where I see this truth and feel it to my bones, I quickly forget.

When I'm in the middle of the mess, when life is delivering blow after blow, when Satan is whispering lies, when I'm on my knees, not even in prayer, just debilitated by the heaviness of that season and too weighed down to stand, the knowledge that Jesus can redeem everything and is working all things together for good doesn't *feel* very good. I acknowledge that. But He still is. Whether I lean into it or not.

So, whether you're on the mountaintop surveying all He's done, or in the valley, asking God when He'll lift you out of the pit, He is healing you. He is redeeming the broken things in your life. He is bringing beauty from ashes. Because Jesus heals. You might not see it all right now. If you don't, hang on to this promise (from the most impatient girl out there), Jesus heals, time helps.

Chapter 20

Wicked Impatience

*S*peaking of my impatience … I am not a patient person. I am, in fact, a very impatient person. I've known this since I was little, and while I knew it wasn't something to be proud of, I just accepted it as my nature, my 'forever struggle' sin, my thorn in the flesh. If Paul had one, surely the rest of us were bound to have one (or several) too, right?

Over the years I've seen that my impatience causes me, and others around me, pain. But I didn't really see it as something big enough to change. Okay, that's a lie. I've never had any decent justification for this particular sin, I just didn't want to have to learn patience. Because I realized (later than I should have) that learning patience would require a circumstance that **requires** patience. I mean patience isn't something if I pray hard enough, God just one day, **BOOM**, gives me patience. And then I am a serene patient person. Unfortunately, that's not how it works.

If I'm going to be a patient person, it's going to be because I learned patience. And unfortunately, learning patience is going to try my patience.

I know that because I'm in it. Recently God has convicted me that my impatience needs to change. Not only because it hurts me and others around me, but because my impatience actually hinders my ability to walk with God in what He's doing. When I demand to see things on my own timeline, God can't invite me into the rest of what He wants to show me. Because I don't give Him space to move. Or time to weave eternity into my reality.

I'm in the learning process. There's something God has placed on my heart that He's doing – something I am not to push or prod along, to simply trust He's got it. And I've actually been leaning into the lesson for the most part, leaning into trust, leaning into how big God is and how He can do anything, even this. And I have even felt peace in my practice of patience.

Until I revert back to impatience. Until I decide God hasn't moved fast enough, and I should check in on His progress. And almost as immediately as I want to check in, I feel my spirit sour. I'm realizing my impatience actually robs me of joy.

My wanting to intervene causes me to immediately doubt God. It causes me to rush ahead and believe God is not moving (or not moving fast enough) so I need to get involved. I need to help. I need to at least check in and make sure the situation is making progress. And there have been times where God has prevented me from doing so. He's literally held me back. While this should be a sign that He's got it and is trying to gift me something without my efforts, instead my impatience has caused my heart to think of all the scenarios in which God might not only **NOT** be doing what I've been believing He's doing, but in fact, that this situation might be taking a turn for the worse.

Why do I go to worst-case scenarios so quickly? Because my heart is sinful. My heart is impatient. My soul is untrusting. I want everything now. (Actually, yesterday would be nice.) And because I like having control (or at least deluding myself into believing I have control). It feels less scary.

But, with a few grey hairs that my stylist gracefully covers, God is finally showing me that if He actually gave me everything I thought I wanted when I thought I wanted it, my life would be a wreck right now. If He let me strong-arm His will to fit my plans, I'd be pretty unhappy. Off the top of my head, I would be in a soul-sucking job. I would still be avoiding anything 'messy' because my faith didn't go that deep. I would be filled up with the world, and spiritually empty. I would be miserable. So, at 32, I can honestly say "thank you Jesus" for not letting my impatient heart get all it wants when it wants it.

But what about the good things I want? What about the salvation of a friend? The revival of a city? And a spouse to partner with on this journey? I've been praying for these for years, and I still haven't seen them happen. Isn't my hurry okay for these spiritual things? I mean surely if God cared about them too, He'd do them sooner. Right?

God is *slowly* teaching me His timing isn't linear, and won't always make sense to me. I emphasize slowly because I find myself often stubbornly resisting His call to unlearn impatience. I'm not usually a slow learner, but I am taking my sweet time on this one.

Yet God keeps inviting me to learn. And can I tell you – this lesson actually has sweet fruit?

Bear with me, because I'm just a beginner, but I think waiting on God allows me to see Him move. With a couple of months of active waiting under my belt (instead of my usual running out of, in front of, or around any situation requiring patience) and a whole lot of the Spirit working in me, I'm kind of *enjoying* this season of waiting. Not the waiting itself, per se. But as I wait in obedience for what He's spoken, I get to see Him. I get to know Him better. I become more acquainted with His voice, with His rhythms, with His ways.

In the waiting, I'm seeing God.

Faith isn't built with one big decision, but a million little ones. Waiting requires an active faith, and numerous decisions towards obedience. I'm starting to think God asks us to learn patience precisely so we can journey with Him better. Because impatience actually hinders our ability to see what He's doing, and to let Him work on our behalf. I actually think impatience robs us of blessings.

If a friend invited me over for dinner, it would be plain bizarre, if not downright rude, for me to bring my own brown bag dinner and say hey, I brought this as a backup in case you didn't cook, or in case I got hungry before you served the meal. My friend would be hurt, and I would ruin the intimacy of letting them bless me with the meal. But isn't that exactly what I do to God with my impatience?

I tell God over and over that if He doesn't 'perform' on my timeframe, then I'm going to go with my backup plan, my own brown bag dinner, because then at least I won't be hungry. And who knows if He was planning to provide anyway? Because honestly, I almost always have a backup plan. I don't let my trust get me out past my skis. That's dangerous. Then I have to (gulp) **TRUST** God. Come what may.

But what if that's not as scary as it sounds? What if it's an epic adventure? A glorious romance?

God is good. I know that. And I'm finally coming around to believe that God is good to *me*. Which, by the way, I think is one of the most important theological points to get one's head (and heart) around. ***Believing God is good does almost nothing unless you believe God is good to YOU.*** That He is for you. That He is not against you. That He'll move mountains to rescue you. That He's bound up hell to protect you. That's He's weaving pieces of eternity together in your favor.

Perhaps waiting for the Lord isn't a curse but a blessing. Perhaps learning patience is an invitation to see His glory more clearly. Perhaps my impatience is actually bondage from the pits of hell, not a benign sin. I think impatience is one of the greatest lies Satan has spoken to my heart. Because at the heart of my impatience is a mistaken belief that if things don't happen on my timeframe, God isn't good. But that's just not true. As much as it can feel true, it's not.

God's timing is not our timing. My urgency is not His. He isn't beholden to my timetables because He is outside of time. He isn't limited by the calendar.

So, slowly …. *slowly*, I've begun to release my grasp on my impatience and let Him remold my heart. Let Him speak of eternal glories that are so outside time it's outrageous for me to try to conceive of them within the boundaries of earthly time.

He's got this.

To all my fellow impatient sisters, He's got it. And you. And the future. And the next thing that you'll worry about. He's got it.

And He's inviting us to watch Him handle it. To patiently wait for Him to move, to heal, to restore, to redeem. It's His nature. It's what He loves to do. And He does it so much better than we could.

So step back with me? Let's get out of the driver's seat and climb in the passenger seat. Let's allow Him to drive. Let's remember God isn't an Uber-driver, shuttling us to where we say we need to go. He's God – He's got a better and more creative plan for this road trip than our short-sighted plans could accomplish. We can relax knowing He'll get us to where we need to be, and it's better than what we could have asked for (or planned). Kick off your shoes, put your feet on the dashboard, and enjoy the scenery along the way. It's going to be stunning!

Chapter 21

The Gift of Rest

I am a do-er. A get-things-doner. A planner. A girl who likes to go.

I like to be productive. I like to accomplish things. I like to be active, I like to have a purpose. And I hate feeling lazy. (I've never been accused of being "chill".)

In many ways, being a high achiever has been beneficial in my life thus far.

It's the "right" personality for my job – you've never heard of a "low-key" lawyer. Corporate life in general usually rewards the high achievers. We glamorize tech moguls who didn't sleep for 10 years getting their companies off the ground. We attend seminars on how to do more work in the limited 24 hours a day we each have. We tell each other to dream bigger, to plan better – to do more. We must go-go-go and do-do-do.

This isn't just true in the corporate world. We do it in our churches and our homes as well. We go-go-go and serve-serve-serve.

(But it's justified as godly in this context.) People depend on us: church members, kids, spouses, parents, siblings. And Christ's love is sacrificial. So, what's a little sacrifice of our time and sleep? We're just being Christ-like. (That's sarcasm, in case it doesn't come through on paper.)

As I'm slowly learning, my busyness and achieving are not as glamorous (or righteous) as I used to think. I'm learning that rest is actually a gift. And God gives abundantly in the margins if I'll stop go-go-going for a second or two.

I had the mixed blessing and curse of not just staying employed during 2020, but having one of the busiest years I hope to ever have work-wise. For whatever reason, my area of law blew up and my firm was crazy busy. Knowing much of the country was out of work because of the pandemic, I felt blessed to have a job.

But I took this gift and made it into something I needed to "earn." I started working like a mad woman to "honor" the gift God gave in sustained employment. I worked and worked and worked. (What else was there to do?) By October, I was shot. I was cranky. I was angry. And I loathed my job.

In a feeble attempt at recharging (my hands booked the plane ticket before I had a chance to think it through), I decided to head back home to Indiana for a week in October to try to decompress and get a change of scenery. I had a counseling session the week before and mentioned to Christine that I was super tired and was heading home to "rest." She asked if I was taking time off work? I said I was planning to still work remotely during this time away. Christine voiced her concern. She said I should actually take the week off of work. Perhaps more. She told me I was burnt out and I needed to rest.

I couldn't take that kind of time off, I told her. That would mean my co-workers had more to do. I couldn't let them down. That would be selfish. Besides, I couldn't imagine not having to work for a whole week (it had been a while since I had really taken an unplugged vacation). What would I do with my time? It was October of 2020, after all, and we were still in the earlier days of a pandemic with limited options to "relax" outside of the home. I protested her suggestion as preposterous, if not impossible.

But something in my spirit knew she was right.

I knew it was a problem if I couldn't take a week off of work. If I felt beholden to my job so much that I felt like I couldn't walk away, maybe it was a *major* problem. After all, I had worked 24/7 at my last company – the whole point of this job had been to not work around the clock and make myself miserable. So, I took a week and a half off work, not even working remotely. And I did so pretty last-minute. That's not necessarily recommended professionally, but I knew I needed it. I spent the first few days still in Colorado decompressing a bit. Remembering what it was like to not work before I went home.

The Saturday before I went home, my best friend's mom died far too young after a hard-fought battle with cancer. I was so grateful to already be headed home and be able to be with her in her time of loss, but needless to say that week didn't turn out to be as restful as I had planned. Honestly, for me, there was nothing restful about 2020.

But I started craving rest. And in 2021, God introduced me to the real gift of rest. And I got to see that He can multiply the margin I give Him.

It started at the beginning of the year. I was burnt out from work, and was disheartened by my employer, knowing it was not a forever home. But instead of jumping to a next job, I felt God's Spirit telling me to wait, to rest, to learn better boundaries there, so that I could carry the next job well.

So, for five months, I kept on keeping on at a job that I knew was not a forever home. But I worked differently. I had boundaries.

I no longer woke up and checked e-mails in bed. I waited until at least 7:30 am to start working. And I stopped around dinner. I didn't volunteer to take on every extra project (especially as my employer was bleeding people due to poor management – I realized it wasn't my job to pick up the slack that poor leadership produced).

I felt great.

My employer was not as thrilled. A few of my superiors voiced recognition that I was no longer allowing myself to be their go-to girl (and not in a "good for you" way). But I didn't care. Which was weird for my people-pleasing self. Though I wasn't actively looking for a new job yet, I knew this was temporary. I knew that this employer would not fire me but was bristling against my new boundaries, and I knew it was an opportunity to learn to work differently, in a place where I had job security.

When I did finally start looking for my next job, I had developed better boundaries, and had had a chance to rethink what I wanted out of a career. I was looking for a place I could exercise a biblical lifestyle with margin. Not a place that demanded my all.

This was no small ask because law firms aren't really known for biblical lifestyles. They're kind of famous for long hours and employees who are wedded to the job. To make it more difficult, my industry was still on fire during the summer of 2021. While I had struggled to get my foot in the door three years prior, now I had my choice of jobs because of a crazy market. (It was weird. And I have to acknowledge, it was 1000% God.)

In the interview process, I had a whole slew of criteria. I didn't want to go certain places because I knew the (poor) reputations of their lawyers. I didn't want to go certain places because I knew the number of billable hours that were expected (too many). I didn't want to go other places because I didn't want to get sucked into a wormhole that asked for my soul in exchange for a paycheck. To say God perfectly lined up a crazy hot market where I could name my terms with teaching me boundaries and giving me a renewed outlook on work is a gross understatement.

It was honestly a miracle.

The place I ended up at impressed me for a few reasons. But honestly, one big reason was the answer I got from the managing director in my initial interview when I asked about taking time off in-between jobs. Again, this was an insane time for my area of law. Everyone, everywhere, was extremely busy. Any request to take time off in-between was going to be a major inconvenience to my future employer. But I asked. I said I was thinking about taking a week off in-between to recharge. And my managing director insisted that I take at least two weeks off.

At the urging of my new HR director, I actually took ***three*** weeks off in-between. Twenty-one days. I was extremely blessed to be able to financially afford to do so, but also blessed to have my employer's support in doing so. I didn't realize how much I needed a break.

I hadn't had three weeks to just **be** in, well, as long as I could remember. I went from undergrad to law school, and law school to the bar exam, and the bar exam to my first job. While I did have a few weeks off when I moved to Denver after my first job, I was also flat broke, so I lived in fear financially, and didn't fully enjoy that time (plus, I didn't have friends in Denver yet, so it was a bit anxiety producing).

This time I had a plan. Week one I would relax in Colorado (my parents were coming for a long weekend to start out my 3 weeks), then I'd do a solo national parks road trip that I'd been wanting to do for two years. The first week went as planned. But everyone and their brother wanted to go to Yellowstone and Grand Tetons and rooms were going for $500+ a night for a Best Western. I'm not a camper (and campsites were booked, too) and I was not about to pay outrageous amounts for what should be a cheap hotel – I knew it would ruin my mood the entire time. So, instead, I booked a week in Florida, along a beach my family frequently visited when I was younger.

Here's the thing – I am not a huge beach vacation person. Don't get me wrong, I like the beach – it's beautiful, but I love mountains and adventure. I don't sit still well. My mom and sister can lay on the beach for hours and hours. I'm bored after about one.

But God knew I didn't need more plans, or more adventures – I just needed rest. So I went to Florida and sat on the beach. By myself.

I read. I biked. I swam. I ate. I prayed. I tanned. I sat in rainstorms (which were a welcome reprieve from Colorado wildfires), and I slept. A lot. That's about it. I had planned to write large portions of this book on that trip and wrote next to nothing.

I had no energy to do anything productive. I needed to just exist.

I'll be honest, I felt selfish spending money on myself to be by myself on a beach. It felt too extravagant. It felt wasteful.

But it also required faith. Faith to lean into rest. To literally be stuck in a place to rest. And it felt like a small faith step that perhaps this would be the last chance I'd ever have to take this kind of trip and have this kind of space to rest on my own. Perhaps my next career move would occur when I had a husband and/or kiddos, and I wouldn't be able to just run away for a week and sleep. So, I took advantage of the opportunity God gave me. And I look back at that time so fondly. It was refreshing for my soul.

Not because I did anything impressive. Honestly, not even because I got some great revelation from God sitting on the beach. (I didn't.) Just because I got to breathe.

I am usually looking for something productive to justify my existence, but that week, God reminded me He doesn't need my productivity. Like, at all.

As I got back to Colorado and began preparing to start my new job, I decided to work differently from the get-go. I was not going to give my job 100% of my energy, let alone the old adage of giving 110%, for two reasons. First, because I have a whole life. I am not my job, and I don't define myself by being a lawyer. If I give 100% to my job (as I had done with my prior firm), I have 0% left to give of myself to anything or anyone else in my life. That's simple math. We are obviously to work as if working for the Lord, but that doesn't involve giving all of our energy to an employer.

My job is to do my job well. To work with excellence. But not perfection. And not without boundaries. As it turns out, I don't have to be the best. As I recall, 90% is still in the "A" range. There's a difference between excellence and being the top dog. I can't think of a single bible verse where God says "be better than everyone." Because frankly, that mindset often leads to pride. And pride blinds us to God's provision – it deludes us into thinking we "earned" what we have. Worse, that we "deserve" it.

I can find myself believing that God's output is a direct result of my input.

That's bad theology. (And generally, a bad way to live.) God doesn't need my production. He doesn't need my work. He uses it, for sure. But He can do just as much (and more) without it. How do I know that?

Because He blew me away with not one, but two knock-my-socks off financial blessings in 2021 that reminded me He not only doesn't need my work, but He'll bless the margin I give Him, because it honors Him, and reminds me He's the one who provides.

Any time you start a new job, there's usually a "ramp-up" period. Even if you're great at your job, people have to start to get to know you (and remember that you're even there) before you get busy, or as lawyers often call it, "full-plated." I was definitely not full-plated the first few months of work. I was actually slow. But a month in, I got an email from management that we were all, **ALL**, getting a "thank you" bonus because the firm was doing so well. This is not at all a common occurrence in law firms generally (nor, as I found out, at this one in particular).

This bonus was generous. Generosity that I did not deserve.

I hadn't been grinding away with this firm for two years during a pandemic. I hadn't been crushing it all summer while they were busy. I was lounging on a beach in Florida! Honestly, part of me thought about e-mailing my director and saying they should disburse my portion amongst other employees, since I didn't earn this bonus.

But I felt convicted that if I did so, I would be throwing away a gift. Not as much a financial gift (although that was awesome), but a thoughtful, intentional gift from my loving Heavenly Father. A gift that revealed two things to me. First, God blesses me because He chooses to, not because I've earned it or deserve it. Second, God multiplies the margin I give Him. I **did not** earn this bonus. But I still got it. And it happened to be almost the exact amount of money I would have made if I had worked for those three weeks that I took off in-between jobs.

That bonus changed my outlook on work even more. Yes, I wanted to work well – and definitely wanted to be a contributing member of the team to a place that I saw was generous even when I didn't deserve it. But honestly, that bonus shattered my idea that I needed to desperately claw my way to earning "more" – financially, relationally, spiritually, any of it. The phrase that defined much of the latter half of 2021 for me was "my input does not determine Your output."

Just to punctuate that, God decided to again wow me at the end of 2021.

I had already gotten a pretty significant raise over the summer due to "adjustments" to deal with a crazy hot market. And then had received the generous "thank you" bonus a month in that I didn't earn. So, I was not expecting much of anything at the end of the year. Besides, I was not a "rockstar" anymore. I was doing well and I liked my firm, but I knew plenty of colleagues who were objectively outperforming me.

So, I walked into my review with seriously low expectations. And when my director told me that I was getting a raise and a bonus, I was surprised. When she told me the amounts, I was blown away. (Good thing we were still required to wear masks at that point because I think my jaw hit the floor.) What made it almost more insane was when I realized it was almost the exact amount of money I thought I deserved at the end of 2020, after a year of busting my butt for a prior employer. (Who had not paid me anywhere close to it.) I was floored.

But what made it more amazing is that I knew, like *knew*, I didn't deserve any of it. Because I hadn't worked harder to "earn" it. I think it was a special year of favor, and lessons in rest. I think God was telling me that He saw me, and saw my efforts and strivings. And wanted me to know that He could provide extravagantly without either. I think God invited me to see that He can do more with less.

While the example in this chapter is based on work and finances, the lesson certainly doesn't stop at my bank account. I think God was trying to teach me rest in my relationships – with Him and with others. I don't need to earn His love. It's there. I just need to soak it in. I don't need to work "harder" to find a husband. I just need to trust that God will provide well in His time, not mine.

Rest is a gift. It's part of a biblical rhythm of life. One of the 10 Commandments is to honor the Sabbath. Sabbath was a day set aside for rest, a day without work, a day to commune with

God. It's a rhythm many of us 21st century believers (especially American believers) seem to ignore. I did for much of my life thus far. But Sabbath matters.

It's a space to stop. To remind myself that God gives without my efforts. To remind myself of who He is and who I am. It's a space to rest. To recharge. Creativity and productivity are easier when my brain is recharged. Life is better in general when my soul is recharged. Many of us look for one long weekend or one vacation to recharge, but this is not the biblical way. We weren't meant to run like the Energizer bunny and only stop long enough to swap out batteries. We're meant to stop regularly. We're meant to put away our efforts, our earning, our striving – regularly. We're meant to go out and enjoy the world, the resources, and the relationships God has provided – regularly.

Rest is a gift. One I'm still unwrapping, but one that keeps getting better the more I embrace it. I see God better when I rest. I am able to gaze longer at His glory when I stop trying to get more of my own. That doesn't mean my life doesn't tempt me to ignore rest. I'm still a lawyer, and work is still busy. There's a daily temptation to give in to the rhythms and patterns of the world around me. But I keep praying my life is now one defined by rest, defined by a rhythm that looks different than many of my peers. And I pray God does exceedingly more with the margin I give Him.

Chapter 22

Blessed, but Still Single

*A*s I write this, I'm still single. And often, I still don't like it. It still aches.

I've always wanted someone to say that in a Christian context. That God is good, they are thankful for what they have, but there's still something missing – and that the missing piece hurts.

I've wanted to hear it before their story got the happy ending. What does it feel like, and look like, when you're still in it? And when you still don't want to be?

God, in His infinite humor, decided that I got to tell that story. My continued story of singleness. My story isn't just singleness "back then". It's my present. I still haven't found my "perfectly imperfect" life partner. (Not for lack of trying and praying and trying some more.) And it hurts. I can't say I'm "okay" with it. I haven't arrived at that divine place of singleness where I'm 100% at peace with it and it's all okay. My faith in God is solid. My trust in Him continues to grow.

I know He's good. I even know He's good to me.

But my singleness still doesn't always feel good. (Honestly, most of the time it doesn't feel good.) And I haven't come to a place where I've accepted it could last forever, though I've asked God for that type of peace and acceptance.

I get by most days. I even get by well most days. I've filled my life – I have good employment, good friends, an amazing church, and fun hobbies.

But sometimes the ache – the longing – feels overwhelming. Even when I'm otherwise thriving, I find tears can come like mighty rivers over the longing and lack that my singleness still creates. They came yesterday. I was overwhelmed by my single-ness and the fact I keep getting older and the husband and kiddos have not yet arrived.

Even when it's not tears, there's an ever-present awareness of my singleness lurking behind every corner. When my head hits my pillow at night, I'm alone. When I come home from work, I'm alone. When I travel to see friends and family, I fly alone. When I go to the grocery, I'm shopping for one. My life still does not include a husband or children. And by God's grace, I've come to realize that my life isn't supposed to be centered around my job in the meantime.

But in this season, I often still feel alone. And this alone-ness is usually when the longing pulls hardest. Those moments that yes, I can enjoy by myself, but I think, I'd like to enjoy with someone else. Those places that I've learned to be alone in, but every once in a while, I remember how nice it would be to do together.

Often this remembering of what I still long for, and lack, cre-ates sadness. It's a grief, I think, for where I long to be, and am not. For what I long to have, but don't. It's confusion, too. For where I am, and how powerless I feel to change it. Confusion for why God has continued to allow it. Confusion for why finding a partner has been so hard for me. Confusion as to why it's still the longing that is deepest.

I know a lot of Christian people who will tell you that if you don't have something you want, maybe it's an idol. Jesus is enough.

Yes, Jesus is enough. I truly believe that. And at times finding a spouse has been an idol. But, I've also asked God repeatedly to take away the desire if He isn't going to provide for me in that way. And He hasn't taken it away.

My deepest earthly longing is to find my spouse – my forever partner for this journey called life. I've known that for a long time. But re-realized that a few months ago. When I found myself journaling that I want to be a wife more than I want to be a mom. Maybe that makes me terrible, but it's true. I want a partner. I want a husband. I want someone to go on adventures with. To make dinner with. To ski and hike with. To build a home with. To share my hopes and dreams with. To serve. To love. To cuddle. These are desires I can't seem to shake.

I want a good man. A godly man. A strong man. A man of honor and integrity. A man with conviction. A man with determination. A man whose humor brightens my days. A man whose arms hold me tight and protect me from the mess of the world. (And I wouldn't mind if those arms were covered in tattoos, since I'm still waiting and dreaming.)

I want the relationship. I want my best friend. Someone to do all of life with. Someone who I get to cheerlead and encourage.

To love and serve. To get dressed up for. To wear sweats and sleep in with. (And "sleep with" – definitely that, too.)

I want romance and leadership. I want my perfectly imperfect husband.

But he hasn't arrived yet. God hasn't delivered him yet. And I have lots of questions about why. I wish my Mr. was by my side as I wrote this. I wish I got to tell the story of waiting turned to provision. Of God's double-portion style goodness. While I wish my present was different than it is, I know God has purpose in it.

Honestly, when I got serious about writing this book, I knew I'd be single writing it. I actually didn't want a man to interrupt this process, because something in my soul knew I needed to be "in it" to speak to the rest of you who are "in it" and also feel alone. Who need to hear that yes, there is pain, but hope is still possible in the messy middle – in the waiting, in the desert.

What God has for you, has been reserved for you. I pray this book is part of what God has for you. It's part of what God has for me. And I truly believe it's part of my *why*. Why God has allowed this season. This long season. This hard season. The questions and confusion that ensued. The pain and the healing that have come with it and through it. And the deep conviction that God is purposefully writing my story.

God loves me more than I can even imagine. If I'm still single, it's because He has a plan – for my singleness, and hopefully, for my future marriage. And I do believe (and continue to pray) He'll hold every tear I shed as my earthly understanding lags behind His eternal purposes.

Chapter 23

Streams in the Desert
(or Ski Lifts in a Pandemic)

*S*ometimes God knows how fried I am. How burnt out and tired I am. And He gives life-giving places to my parched soul.

He literally gave Elijah streams in a desert.

He gave me ski lifts in a pandemic.

I learned how to ski while dating Daniel but didn't immediately catch the bug. The first year I lived in Colorado, I was too busy, and honestly, too depressed to want to try skiing again. When my second full winter rolled around, I decided I'd invest in a ski pass (which is no small expense) and really dive in. But I was too busy at work to ski in 2019. I made it once in January of 2020 and was hoping for a late ski season when COVID closed the slopes and made that hope a dashed dream.

While that was disappointing at the beginning of 2020, it became a blessing in 2021. Since I had only skied once on my

2019-2020 pass, my 2020-2021 pass was pretty inexpensive as resort operators were desperately trying to lure people back to the slopes while COVID was still a daily reality. Their plan worked for me. I decided to buy a dirt-cheap pass and really go all in knowing it would be the most inexpensive ski season I'd ever have.

The first day I skied was at the end of 2020. I was still scared – I was afraid I was going to fall and break my leg (or my face). I had learned to ski as an adult after all, and there's something about going face first down a mountain on skis that screams "danger." But the second day, I hit my stride. And then I was hooked.

Friends had told me that a day just comes in skiing where you're free – you aren't thinking about your technique, you're not afraid – you're just flying. As an over-thinker, I thought that would never happen for me. But it did. On my first ski day in 2021. In Breckenridge, Colorado.

I was flying. I was unafraid. And I was thrilled!

Skiing became my outlet in 2021. Because of COVID, the slopes weren't as busy as they typically are. And because a pandemic raged on, the people at the slopes were, for the most part, people like me who had already decided to live with some risk and get out of the house to stay sane. It was a unique blessing that I tried to acknowledge at the time but can only fully appreciate later.

I had long days and long weekends on the slopes. Just me and the mountains – with fresh powder and the God who put them all there. If you've never been skiing in Colorado in winter, let me tell you, it's incredibly beautiful. Honestly, it's stunning.

Looking back, I think how gracious of God to give me beauty in what felt like the true armpit of the pandemic. When I was beyond weary. Ridiculously tired. Overwhelmed by the continued state of chaos. In that space, God gave me a place where my brain turned off and my eyes were fixed on beauty. Skiing was my happy place.

I felt safe.

I felt free.

I felt hope.

There's something about standing on a mountain for me that changes my mood and my outlook. I just can't be mad or sad or down on a mountain. Because every time I see mountains or stand on one, I'm reminded that my God created these monstrous beauties, and can tear them down with a single word.

I'm reminded these towering giants have been around for a long time before me, and they'll likely be around for a long time after. I'm reminded that my God has seen every day of their existence. He has watched over them. He has noticed every stray rock, every avalanche, every drop of rain that has touched this dirt. And if He notices all of this, and commands all of it, then I think I'm in good hands.

God gave me a physical space to know deeply that if He needs to move a mountain on my behalf, He can. A physical space to remember that He can provide good things even in the darkest of days. A physical place to see His beauty on display.

In 2021, skiing reminded me of this, and brought my soul back to life. It didn't make all of the crap of life go away. But it gave me a get-away. A place to breathe. A place to recall God's power, His beauty, and His intimate love of me. It gave me enough to carry on. To keep going when the world around me wasn't getting better. To seek out His long-term goodness, and to remember His faithfulness in prior seasons.

Skiing refreshed me. It created a sanctuary of sorts. A place to recall His power, His goodness, and His attention to beauty.

But even at the streams (or ski lifts), God has things to teach us. Skiing gave me refuge, but it also provided a lesson. A place to learn that leaning in to the scary can produce more joy than I thought possible. But I have to be willing to face my fear, and I have to be willing to keep getting back up.

As previously mentioned, I learned how to ski as an adult, which is much harder than learning as a kid. Kids are fearless and their center of gravity is pretty low, so falling usually doesn't scare them much. If you're a rational human being learning to ski as an adult, the prospect of falling scares you. And usually, as a beginner, you'll do anything you can to avoid it. You tense up, you lean back, you squeeze your legs into "pizza" as forcefully as you can – anything to stay upright and in control.

But, in skiing (and in life), you expend more energy trying to avoid falling than just relaxing and risking a fall. In skiing, to avoid falling your body naturally wants to lean uphill (aka backward) – to stay closer to perceived safety. But to have any real control on your skis, you actually have to lean **downhill**. Into the scary. And into the impending fear of falling.

For most of us, you have to actively tell your brain to do this, to lean into gravity. As you lean downhill, you tend to go faster. It's terrifying at first, but once you do it a few times, it's a little thrilling. Once you're a decent skier, going fast is fun. I now love racing down the slopes. I just spent a week doing it and I felt alive.

But even though I'm no longer a novice skier, I still fall sometimes. Not **because** of the speed; usually because I hit a bump or a twig, and with the speed and the right angle, those bumps or twigs hit different, and I fall. I realized this week that when I fall, fear can creep back in. I notice I want to go slower the next run. Falling makes me forget that I know how to ski – falling makes me want to retreat back into perceived safety and stop leaning downhill. But I'm not safer skiing scared. I'm not safer leaning back uphill. I'm just scared.

I think this journey with God is kind of like that, too. To really get to that sweet spot of intimacy with God, you have to lean in. But leaning in means getting out of your comfort zone, and risking getting knocked down sometimes. Life will knock you down. Satan will knock you down. But that doesn't mean leaning into God's goodness and promises is a bad idea. I was talking to my best friend about this a few days ago (txting actually, since she lives a thousand miles away), and said "I keep getting a little bolder every time I get back up after getting knocked down. I guess in some ways my prayer isn't that I won't get knocked down, but that I bounce back up faster each time."

Skiing has brought me tremendous joy and made me a little more willing to get back up when I get knocked down, because I know the thrill of the downhill is worth the risk.

My prayer for you is that when you go through the desert seasons (which, you inevitably will) that God gives you your own streams or ski lifts. That He gives you something that refreshes you and gives you a joy beyond your situation. Maybe it's a new hobby. Maybe it's a new friend. Maybe it's an old passion rediscovered. I pray He teaches you new lessons while you're enjoying the refreshment your stream provides. Whatever it is, I pray fresh water finds you in those grey, dreary seasons of the soul.

The desert can be dry. It can be barren. It can feel endless. But there's still hope in the desert. Streams of water for our parched souls. And ski lifts in the midst of a pandemic.

Chapter 24

Saying Yes to God

The title of this chapter seems a little cliché, I know. Many of us are Jesus-followers, so of course we say "yes" to God. But, do we really?

Do we really say "yes" to all of God? To His plan, not ours? I ask this with no judgment, only honesty.

I'm realizing lately that for most of my life, I've said "yes" to God ... with a back-up plan. Or I've said yes to God and gone ahead and tried to accomplish His will ... without Him. Anyone else? I was talking to friends about this last night – saying "yes" without a backup plan requires crazy trust. Even for us Jesus-followers. Trust without a Plan B – surely that's reserved for those next-level believers – true heroes of the faith. Noah, Abraham, David, Esther. Not normal, everyday, 21st century women.

Right?

Lately I've been convicted the answer is "wrong" – that the spiritual realms are brimming with activity and God is just waiting for me to say I'm willing to see things not with my own two eyes, but with spiritual eyes. Waiting for me to be willing to actively put off my flesh and actively put on the Spirit. Waiting for me to get deeper into the waters of faith.

I'll be honest with you, I've been resisting this invitation for a while now. Probably years.

Listen, I love Jesus – I'm so thankful for a God who is active and present and powerful. But was I ready to be ***that*** Christian? You know, the woman who has a presence about her where you just ***know*** that she hears from God? Where she has so many stories of God's faithfulness that you can't help but be moved by God's goodness? If I'm being honest, I didn't want to be that person.

I wanted to be "normal." I wanted to have the nice slightly-above-average American dream. Nice career (check), which I would put on hold for a while when the right man came along and we'd have a nice marriage and nice kids and live in a nice neighborhood and be friends with everyone on the block and be involved in our local church. This is all good. And it still might be the story God writes for me. But I don't think He wants me to be "normal" even in this type of "nice and normal" setting.

I think He's got more for me to see and experience of Him than "normal." But if that's His call, it will require my trust. And obedience.

That's where the rubber meets the road.

As we get towards the end of this book, and as I near the end of my writing of the same, God has been pricking my heart with an uncomfortable question, which is simply this – ***am I asking the right questions***?

If I'm being honest with myself, I think most of my 32 years on earth have been defined by telling God what I want and asking Him to do it. And honestly, He's said yes to many of those things. Sometimes not how I expected, but in many instances, I got to where I asked to be.

I was able to go to law school even without a 4.0 undergraduate GPA. I got to the salary goal I had as a lawyer at 27. I got to live in downtown areas and have cute apartments. I've been given several "dream" jobs. And I know God both had and has purpose in those things – the lessons they've taught and the blessings they've bestowed.

But I think God is asking me to start asking different questions.

I think God is asking for a disciple, not a manager. As a prayer partner recently reminded me, "God doesn't need partners, He needs followers." I'm not going to lie, that pricked my pride a bit. I like working on a team, being a team player, and contributing to a project as an equal. And I'm pretty good at managing projects. But God doesn't need a manager. He actually doesn't need direction at all.

God doesn't **need** anything. He just **desires** my "yes."

Rather than, "hey God, this is what I want, can you do it?" I think I'm being invited to ask "God, what are You doing?" "How can I be involved?" I think instead of telling Him the adventure I am ready to go on, He's asking me to seek out His adventure for me and say "yes" before I even know what it is. I think He's asking me to release my grasp and open my hands to receive His bigger and better plans.

But, can I be honest? I'm more of a Jonah than a Noah.

I'm far more likely to run from what God is calling me to than faithfully, patiently obey long before I see the fulfillment of His word come to pass. The question I've begun to wrestle with in this space is "how long?" How long will I build a boat with no rain in sight? How long will I faithfully wait on the Lord, and continue in whatever direction He leads, until I see the destination? Will I veer off course after Mile 2 because I'm not there yet? Or will I wait patiently? With hope?

I like adventures. And I like destinations. The older I get, the more I see that the best adventures take time and are less about the destination than the journey. (Which my earthly father has been trying to tell me for years – sorry I'm slow Dad.)

What if this faith walk is actually the same way? What if God, in His romantic heart, is writing a far better story than I could think to ask for, but while He sees it from beginning to end, He's inviting me to experience it step by step?

God does invite me into the grandeur of His glory, but am I willing to follow Him for more than 24 hours along that path, let alone for years, to see Him do what He says He'll do?

More and more I pray my answer is 'yes'. Instead of asking Him to remove the mountain, I want to have faith to praise Him when the mountain is in the way, knowing He'll lift me up or remove the mountain, in due time. Instead of asking for answers now, I want faith that is willing to hope before I see the answer, before I see His word come to pass.

Lately I've seen that God desires to bless our obedience to big faith. Not always with answers, but with more of Himself. The Bible tells us that as we obey, as we ask for spiritual eyes to see, the Spirit reveals to us even "the deep things of God." (1 Corinthians

2:10.) I want to be a woman God can reveal those things to. I want to be a woman who walks with Him, even in the in-between. Between here and that promised land. I want to say "yes" before I know what the promised land is. Because I think that's actually the point of the journey.

The destination isn't a place, it's a person. The journey isn't toward an object, but toward a relationship. As uncomfortable as it is, I want to be a person who enjoys the journey. Who is present in the journey, and less concerned about the destination. I want to want to know His heart more than I want His blessings. I want to be a woman who says "yes" to God.

I'm not there yet. And probably won't be entirely this side of eternity, but I want to be. Because I think God has a lot He wants to show me if I'm just willing to say "yes."

Chapter 25

The Vulnerability of Hope

Hope is scary. There, someone finally said it. **HOPE – IS – SCARY.**

Yes, hope is good and holy and necessary and even command-ed in Scripture. I know that. And I want to understand hope as this glorious anchor, an other-worldly balm for my soul.

But if I'm honest, often, hope is scary. Because hope is vulnerable.

Hope exposes the distance between where I am and where I long to be, between what I have, and what I am still waiting for. And by admitting the longings, the prayers that have yet to be answered, my soul faces the reality of the unknown. Of "what ifs"? Perhaps the most terrifying aspect is one that is difficult to verbalize – as I see the distance between what I hope for and what I have, I am forced to face a God who allows this distance.

Who *is* God when my prayers are unanswered? Is God *work-ing* when my prayers are unanswered? Does God *care* about my longings? Is God **good** in the space between the deepest longings of my heart and the not-yet-answered requests I present to Him?

In this season of my life, I am still hoping for a wonderful husband – for a partner for the journey, a father to a brood of kiddos, and someone who I can't wait to jump into bed with every night. But as I pen these words, that is a longing that feels very distant. And as I hope is clear as we come to the end of this book, God and I have wrestled over this distance.

In the middle of the reality of my singleness and my deep desire for a good man and a family of my own, doubt has become an unwelcome companion. As has anger. There are some gaps between what I long for and what I have where my actions have caused delays (it's taken a while to lose my COVID weight because I kept eating Crumbl cookies on the regular). But other gaps are simply the natural progression of time. (I couldn't be an adult when I was 10 because 10 isn't adulthood.) I think my singleness falls into the latter category.

I didn't do something wrong to still be here. And God **could** resolve it. Immediately, if He wanted to.

God could deliver a man to my doorstep if He wanted (I mean between all the UPS, Fed-Ex, Amazon, and Grubhub deliveries I had in 2020, that was definitely a possibility). And I have spent plenty of time on dating apps "putting myself out there" and giving God the space to provide.

But He hasn't. At least, not yet.

And honestly, my deepest fear is that He won't. That I will end up forever alone. I want to say I'm mature and godly enough to be okay with that, to say that forever singleness would be well with my soul. But it's still not. Not for lack of trying, I've asked

God to take away the longing if a husband and family is not in my future, or, at least to minimize the depth of the longing.

But so far, He has done neither.

So instead, I sit with this longing that exposes me, and the space between my reality and that longing.

That exposure is vulnerable. *If* I let it be. It can carve space in my soul to let God into my deepest feelings, into very intimate fears. To let Him speak to my heart there. If nothing else, I think God enjoys that – I think He longs for the invitation to be in those nooks and crannies of my heart.

Our God is so beautifully relational, but I often treat Him as a magic genie, or a distant ruler, or sometimes, nothing at all. Many of us have plenty of head knowledge of God, Jesus and the Holy Spirit, but we don't know them personally. We haven't allowed ourselves to need to.

For a long time, I was one of those people.

But God longs to be desired. To be needed. To be trusted. As we all do in good relationships. And perhaps He sometimes allows distance between what I have and what I long for to force me to look at Him. To invite me to get to know Him. To invite me to get to know myself. To invite me to dream with Him.

Often, my dreams and longings are too small. I've already seen this play out in my life. At 32, I see that many of the career dreams I had in my 20s were small. And God, in His glorious wisdom, has invited me to dream bigger. Perhaps my dreams for a future spouse and family are too small, too. I've wanted a good man. A Godly man. An equal. And those are all good things. But maybe, God wants more. Maybe, as C.S. Lewis said, I'm "far too easily pleased." I thought my ministry would just be through my professional life, but maybe it's more. I want a good man to marry, maybe God wants to give me His best.

Maybe I'm asking God for good, and He wants me to ask for extravagant. This is the same God who is able to do "exceedingly beyond" all I can ask for or imagine, right? (Ephesians 3:20). So maybe He hasn't said "yes" yet because my asks are too small. And maybe He hasn't said "yes" yet because delivery now would be premature. Perhaps He's still putting all the finishing touches on the provision and really does desire to give me something more wonderful than I'm asking for.

So, if I'm really brave, I lean into the "not yet" and ask for extravagant. And then wait for God to provide. The waiting is the hardest part for me. Anytime I'm forced to wait, I often assume the worst. I assume that the waiting will bring disappointment. That the thing waited for won't happen.

That is, at the heart of it, why I'm so impatient. I think waiting = disappointment. But that's not God's mathematical equation.

Actually, God + waiting = fruit.

God + vulnerability = beauty.

God + time = miracles.

So, I wait. And I hope in this desert. And I pray that the space in between here and what I'm hoping and praying for reveals beauty, bears fruit, and maybe, just maybe, that I get to see a miracle or two as I hope for things not yet seen.

Notes

Page 71: Soeiro, Loren, "7 Essential Psychological Truths about Ghosting", *Psychology Today*, https://www.psychologytoday.com/us/blog/i-hear-you/201902/7-essential-psychological-truths-about-ghosting.

Page 84: "Signs of a Sociopath: What to Look For." *WebMD*, www.webmd.com/mental-health/signs-sociopath.

Page 120: Chapman, Gary D. *Anger: Taming a Powerful Emotion.* Moody Publishers, 2015.

Page 122: C.S. Lewis' *"The Screwtape Letters"*, Tony Evans' *"Victory in Spiritual Warfare: Outfitting Yourself for the Battle"* and Priscilla Shirer's *"The Armor of God"* are books you should read; with wisdom I'm forever indebted to as they've shaped my understanding of the battle around me.

Evans, Tony. *Victory in Spiritual Warfare.* Harvest House Publishers, 2011.

Lewis, C. S. *The Screwtape Letters.* Tingle Books, 2021.

Shirer, Priscilla. *The Armor of God.* LifeWay Press, 2022.

Page 178: Lewis, C. S. *The Weight of Glory.* William Collins, 2013.

Acknowledgments

First and foremost, I want to thank God for the ability to write this book – the experiences, the thoughts, the time, and the resources to do so. This is all by Him and through Him and my deepest desire is that He receives glory through this endeavor and that women's souls are healed with new insight from His loving heart.

Second, I want to thank Christine. This book would not exist without her. I would not have thought to write it without her gentle, consistent promptings. And I would not have been in a place to write it without her grace and wisdom in my healing journey. I'm so thankful for her guidance and pray this book shows others that healing is possible and good counselors are a literal godsend. Whatever God does through this book, I pray she feels the blessing ten-fold.

A big shout out and heartfelt thanks to my inner circle who reviewed and edited initial drafts of this book – Dad, Kimberli, Christine, Mom, Andrea – I appreciate your care and wisdom!

Thank you to my prayer circle who have prayed over this book and encouraged me along the way.

Thank you to my team at Palmetto Publishing for guiding me through the publishing process.

Thank you to Aria Pickett for capturing my smile after a week that brought nothing but tears.

And a final thank you to my future husband – if you were already by my side, this book would not exist. While I'll continue to pray you come soon, I'm thankful for the lessons I've learned on this side of marriage, and pray they bless "us" when that day comes.

Milton Keynes UK
Ingram Content Group UK Ltd.
UKHW022015160823
426999UK00017B/140/J

9 798822 919198